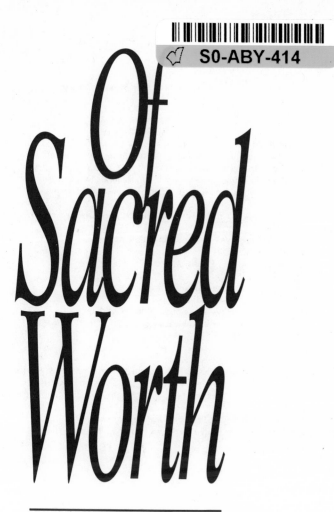

# Of Sacred Worth

## Paul A. Mickey

Abingdon Press
Nashville

241
MJC

*Copyright © 1991 by Abingdon Press*

*This book is printed on recycled, acid-free paper.*

**Library of Congress Cataloging-in-Publication Data**
Mickey, Paul A., 1937-
    Of sacred worth / Paul A. Mickey.
      p.   cm.
    Includes bibliographical references.
    **ISBN 0-687-28405-8 (alk. paper)**
      1. Homosexuality—Religious aspects—Christianity.
    2. Homosexuality—Biblical teaching. I. Title.
BR115.H6M53 1991
241'.66—dc20                            91-6681

*To Jim Thompson*

# CONTENTS

# ACKNOWLEDGMENTS

My deep professional respect is extended to Professors James M. Efird and D. Moody Smith of Duke University Divinity School for their loving and helpful criticism and suggestions, especially regarding the biblical texts.

Among those whose valuable assistance is part of this book are the families and individuals I have counseled, the students at Duke University Divinity School whose discussions and research have educated me, my colleagues at the Divinity School and across the Christian church.

Of special help have been the suggestions and support offered during the initial stages of the project by Dr. Herbert Anderson of Chicago Theological Seminary, the Reverend Jeanne Parsons of Denver University Campus Ministry, and Catherine Ramsey, a graduate student at Duke University Divinity School. Of singular assistance has been the encouragement of Ginny W. Ashmore in her timely cajoling and meticulous transcribing of my words and thoughts.

My wife, Jane Mickey, more so than anyone else, puts up with my various writing projects and encourages me to finish at least part of what I begin. My children, Bruce and Sandi, have lovingly chastised me for plunging into more theological controversy than they ever thought of as rebellious teenagers. My family, like many others who acknowledge the need for this study, understand the need for the church to better serve its Lord and the world.

Finally I want to acknowledge Duke University, which afforded me a sabbatical in Spring 1988 that allowed me to complete advance preparation of this manuscript.

# PREFACE

Perhaps no other contemporary issue holds the Christian church so firmly in its grasp as the torturous debate over homosexuality. The discussion is primarily theological, but the practical implications are manifold: Should a church employ a gay or lesbian youth leader? Dare I or my family member come out of the closet? Should a congregation invite gay couples to worship? Should a worship committee—or a denomination—prohibit a pastor from marrying a gay couple? What about church leaders who are homosexual? Does the Bible in fact give guidance on homosexuality? Does God create men and women only to be straight? Should a bishop prohibit a pastor from blessing the union of a lesbian couple?

A listing of the painful dilemmas that split families, congregations, and denominations could be compounded. The confusion, frustration, debate, sensitivity, and caring continues. Is there any possible way to come to a fuller understanding of the biblical and pastoral perspectives on our human sexuality, especially as they may guide our understanding of homosexuality and heterosexuality and their proper relationships?

This book will not resolve all the questions or end the debate. But it is intended to place the heartache and theological debate into a perspective that offers both biblical and pastoral assistance. A mature response to the issue of homosexuality in the life of the church does not rest solely on biblical passages; nor is it resolved by an appeal to what the church may have always done; and certainly the findings of the social sciences do not by themselves bring resolution to the problem.

Theological, biblical, traditional, and contemporary perspectives help us to pull the pieces of this complex puzzle together. Then the hard part begins: What do I as a Christian actually believe and what should I do to be a faithful witness in offering pastoral and spiritual care for people who are gay or lesbian and for those whose lives are directly touched by friends and family members who are gay or lesbian?

More difficult is the decision as a member of a community of faith to engage in public debate regarding homosexuality, the church, and a Christian lifestyle.

Finally, the practical aim of this study: to offer help for Christians to be faithful followers of our Savior, Jesus Christ, who was both compassionate and uncompromising in his life and witness. My hope is that this study will be both a source and resource to reassure and challenge new insights for compassionate ministry and witness.

A note about language: Language about this issue is in flux. Some people are indeed offended by the use of the word *homosexual,* but it is used in this volume interchangeably with *homophile* and *gay and lesbian* or *gay,* as appropriate.

# PART I

# A THEOLOGICAL PERSPECTIVE

# CHAPTER 1

# We Are Sexual Beings

We are sexual beings and sexuality is good. The theological invitation of this study is to develop a deeper appreciation for God's gift of our sexuality. If we fail first to understand human sexuality theologically, then all discussion about homosexuality is wide of the mark.

We begin our theological exploration of how we as God's children are to express our sexuality. Four steps present themselves for our theological understanding. First, we need to accept ourselves as sexual beings. Second, we need to appreciate that God is glorified in our sexuality. Third, we need to accept the theological truth that God too is a sexual being. Finally, we need to understand that Christian sexuality transcends any claim for a license to justify "if it feels good and sexy, go ahead!"

## Our Sexuality

Associating human sexuality with the act of sexual intercourse limits its scope. For the lower animals, sex correctly is limited to the instinct or drive to mate seasonally for the purpose of procreation. But in the Bible, Genesis 1 and 2 remind us that humanity is the highest order of creation. We are given dominion over all other forms of creation, including their instinctive sex drives. Our dominion and stewardship over creation call us not to exploit or suppress but show loving, responsible expression of our power, including our sexuality.

We are invited to receive God's gift of sexuality and enjoy our sexuality in three ways.

**1.** We need to *receive* our sexuality. We are neither driven by nor frozen into the automatic, instinctual sexual behavior that is characteristic of lower beings. Our sexual behavior is far less predictable and more imaginative than that of other beings. Sex can be more satisfying and certainly more complicated for humans than for the rest of creation. God's gift of sexuality is ours to use and enjoy responsibly, or we may choose to injure others in the misuse of this gift. God's gift of sexuality does not guarantee proper behavior. In accepting the gift of sexuality, we receive sex as one aspect of God's intention for us to enjoy all of creation.

**2.** We are to *enjoy* our sexuality, to find satisfaction in sex, and to have fun. God invites us to engage in our sexuality with a joy unknown among other creatures. As someone has noted, "If God didn't intend us to enjoy our sexuality, God would not have given us so much of it!"

**3.** With God's help, we are expected to *manage* the complex nature of our sexuality. The "breath of life" that God gives in Genesis 2 is a biblical witness that humans are similar to God, being more complex and creative than all other creatures. We have great freedom in and high expectations for enjoying and using wisely God's gift of life.

We may learn some things about human sexuality from the playful sexual behavior of lower animals. However, if we are to understand human sexuality and God's will for us, we look toward God (Psalm 8) not the lower animals for guidance on responsible sex.

### God Is Glorified in Our Sexuality

As sexual beings, how we live out our "breath of life" and our sexuality is a matter of supreme value and importance to

God. All of God's other creatures fall into fairly predictable
orbits of behavior. Only the human spirit has the freedom to
live in a way that either glorifies or disgraces God. There are
three ways we may see God glorified in our human sexuality:

**1.** *God Is Creator.* God is God, the Alpha and the Omega,
the beginning and the end of life. God is to be glorified in all
things, including our sexuality. We may conceive of God as
purely spiritual and consider sex a purely physical act. In fact,
we often refer to sexual intercourse as having carnal knowledge. To link God the creator with sex and the physical may be
difficult for some. But God is creator of spirit and body and
calls us to wholeness and unity of body and spirit, through
Jesus Christ. Jesus, God incarnate, is *the* witness that God is
God of the physical as well as the spiritual. One aspect of
Jesus' call to Christian discipleship is integration of our spiritual desires and our sexual desires. Ours is a call away from
the alienation or rejection of sexuality and toward being a
Christian.

**2.** *My Experience Is Not God.* As Christians we do not have
theological permission to appeal to "my experience" as the
final authority in matters either of life or faith. We may like sex
and adore our sexuality, or we may distrust sex and be turned
off by anything sexual. In the midst of our personal, psychological reactions to our sexuality, God through Christ continues to
call us to wholeness in our sexuality. We may lack wholeness,
either by withdrawing from our sexuality or by overindulging
our sexual impulses. Under these circumstances our experience
is the focal point of our attention, and we forget that God calls
us to a life that allows us to glorify God through our sexuality.
By the same theological understanding, we are not to play God
with our sexuality. We are not created to use our sexuality to
satisfy only our desires.

C. S. Lewis writes about the theological arrogance of sexual
activity that is self-serving in his theological observations about
masturbation:

For me the evil of masturbation would be that it takes an appetite which, in lawful use, leads the individual out of himself to complete (and correct) his own personality in that of another (and finally in children and even grandchildren) and turns it back; sends the man back into the prison of himself, there to keep a harem of imaginary brides. And this harem, once admitted, works against *ever* getting out and really uniting with a real woman. . . . Among those shadowy brides he is always adored, always the perfect lover; no demand is made on his unselfishness, no mortification ever imposed on his vanity. In the end, they become merely the medium through which he increasingly adores himself. . . . After all, almost the *main* work of life is to *come out* of ourselves, out of the little, dark prison we are all born in. Masturbation is to be avoided as *all* things are to be avoided which retard this process. The danger is that of coming to *love* the prison.[1]

Sex is more than a physical act or behavior; and as C. S. Lewis suggests, it is intended to be more than the self-adoration and self-containment dynamics noted about masturbation. Such behavior does not pull us out of the prison of our own "shadowy brides," and we fail to find completion in the sexual other that has the potential to lead to the further fulfillment of children and grandchildren. Sex implies a relationship. God is glorified as we come to experience our sexuality in relation with others and God. Failure to acknowledge the relational nature of sex makes us idolaters. In idolatry the object of worship—in this case sex—is worshiped as the end-all, be-all. Sex may be enjoyable and we are to give thanks to God for creating us as sexual beings. But sexual experience is not God.

**3.** *Fear of Sex Is an Unholy Fear of God.* Several years ago, James Wall, a United Methodist clergy and editor of *The Christian Century,* offered an editorial opinion on sex:

Fear of sex, not desire for it, lies behind the success of the pornography industry. Many adults in our culture are so incapable of establishing intimacy with others that they flee into occasional or compulsive use of pornography—a clinical depiction that erases the mystery.[2]

The fear of receiving the gift of sex and the fear that using our sexual energies will not bring honor and glory to God drive Christians into the clutches of pornography. Preoccupation with pornography is a two-edged sword. One side is the behavior of those actively ensnared in pornographic materials. The other edge is the self-righteous who claim that any explicit sexual imagery or description in print or in electronic media is a violation of sexual propriety. They give vent to their sexual rage and fear of intimacy.

Fear of sex often drives people deeper into the loneliness of nameless sexual partners or into a denial of any social intimacy. Some people fear that if they are not sexually active something is wrong with them. For others, fear of sex keeps them from achieving genuine intimacy with others and with God. Genuine intimacy makes us more comfortable with our own sexuality and increases our capacity to glorify God in the intimacy of spiritual fellowship.

## God Is Sexual

Some people might say the statement "God is sexual" is blasphemous. Perhaps. But to explain this judgment several matters need discussion. Sex was God's idea and creation. As human beings we are sexual beings. In our human sexuality, God participates with us in creation. But it is not an easy relation. We are tempted to run from such spiritual intimacy. This is seen in the age-long battle to spiritualize the faith. A historical theological dilemma for the church is docetism. This doctrine is based on the assumption that God is only a spiritual essence. The Christian affirmation of the Trinity is a statement about God who participates in creation. Surely God is more than sexuality, but in some respect God, as author and finisher of our faith and sexuality, is also a sexual being. God is clearly more than sex, but unless we want to argue that sex comes from somewhere outside God, we must conclude that, in some respect, God also experiences our sexuality. If we take the side that God is in no respect a sexual being, we run the risk of slipping into docetism: we so spiritualize the nature of God that we deny to God any of the physical aspects of creation, including sexuality.

We are called to a multidimensional expression of love and our sexuality. The New Testament passage 1 Corinthians 13 is known as the love chapter of the Bible. It places God's loving relationship with us in a theological perspective and calls us to love in like fashion. What makes this passage so powerful is its stress on freely given, self-sacrificing love. Paul declares that this selfless love is of greater value to God, our neighbors, and ourselves than is faith and hope.

To put this call to love in the context of understanding ourselves as sexual beings, we need to consider several dimensions of love that our English word *love* does not readily communicate. First there is the love of sexual desire itself (*epithymia*). We also have the love of aspiring to gain fulfillment through the sexual partner (*eros*). Another type of love is that of mutuality and friendship (*philia*). Finally, the highest form of human love is the self-sacrificing love that is praised in 1 Corinthians 13 (*agape*).[3]

These four dimensions of love *all* are part of our creation as sexual beings, and in God's great mystery of creation and love each needs the other for fulfillment of the purpose of human life. Paul makes it clear which is the highest level of love (*agape*), but none is separated finally from the other. Pure sexual desire (*epithymia*) finally is inseparable from *agape*. Therefore, God, who in Christ gave us the ultimate gift and demonstration of *agape* love, does not reject the redeeming quality and healthiness of sexual desire.

The high call of *agape* love is to transform *epithymia* into sexual wholeness, as opposed to alienation and abuse. Therefore God is actively transforming all four dimensions of human love and sexuality toward salvation and *agape* through Christ in our lives. God actively works to redeem every aspect of what God has created, including sex. God as creator is a sexual being.

In fact, Episcopal theologian Norman Pittenger borrows an image from Teilhard de Chardin and refers, reverentially, to God as the "cosmic Lover."[4] Pittenger's image connotes God's love for and satisfaction with the very creation God has initiated. The theological concept of God as cosmic Lover is not a diminishment of God's being. It echoes the words recorded at the time of Jesus' baptism: "This is my Son, the Beloved, with whom I am well pleased" (Matthew 3:17).

In the hymn "The Christian Life" by Charles Wesley, the phrase "Jesus, Lover of my soul" is Wesley's way of saying that God through Christ actively participates to woo us and draw near to us. Explicit sexual language is used in scripture and by hymn writers to convey the *agape* love of God. But the words of love in the Christian faith also suggest a kind of spiritually erotic dimension to the intimacy that God shares with us.[5]

Jesus promises the Comforter (the Holy Spirit) to be a lover of the church. As Comforter, Lover, Guide, the Holy Spirit leads us, through Christ, into all truth (John 16:13).

As human beings we are sexual beings and created in God's image. God, in some respects, includes *eros* love in his love for us. If God is love, and not all love is *agape* love, then God also participates in love that is other than *agape* love, namely *eros* and *philia,* and an aspect of *epithymia.*

## Beyond Therapeutic Sexuality

Sexuality is one of God's gifts to us, and it is intrinsically a part of human nature. Our human sexuality is also an aspect of God's nature. While we would assert that sexuality is included in the nature of God, God is not, of course, a purely sexual being. Likewise, as human beings—made in the image of God—we are always more than our sexuality. Sexuality is good. But there are theological limits, restraints, and obligations upon our sexual life. Several aspects of human sexuality threaten theologically to make sex larger than its created intention. I call this threat "therapeutic sexuality."

**1.** *"If It Feels Good, Do It."* The faulty theological message in this catchphrase of therapeutic sexuality is the bad advice that fulfillment of sexual feelings is a fulfilling of human destiny. Many emotions are momentary, all-powerful, and overwhelming: sex, anger, hatred, self-loathing, depression. But there are good reasons for not acting on such feelings. The free, careless, abusive, and exploitive expression of sexuality that we have seen in the past few decades may be on a pendulum swing back toward some degree of balance. The desired balance is the point where sex between human beings is used to express warmth, affection, nurture, and tenderness designed to help the other achieve self-esteem and self-respect (*philia* love). In an editorial in *U. S. News and World Report*,[6] John Leo analyzes the significance of action at the Amherst-Pellham Regional High School in Massachusetts in its enactment of a new sexual harassment code. His concern is over the "schoolhouse puritans" who worry that gossip or a stray glance may be grounds for a sexual harassment charge. The effort to eliminate abusive and alienating sexual expression may have swung too far by denying any kind of sexual expression.

Our theological interest is achieving a balance of sexual expression and restraint in the effort to integrate the four types of love, in the name of Christ. The starting point for healthy expression of sexuality is a frank and open admission that we are sexual beings. In the Amherst-Pellham school effort to stop all sexual harassment, the underlying assumption becomes obvious: we are not sexual beings and any public or publicly overheard expression of *epithymia* is to be denied.

God calls us to a higher level of sexual expression and self-control than to believe sexual "purity" can be legislated. The code of sexual conduct adopted by the Amherst-Pellham school board is the wrong way to address the causes of sexual harassment.

**2.** *Chastity and Singleness.* Mary Meyer of Oak Forest, Illinois, achieved national acclaim in enunciating the guiding principles of the National Chastity Association. For her organization, chastity is a tight channeling of one's sexual behavior: "It disallows kissing, caressing, and even hand-holding until marriage." Of "The Nineteen Desires of Members" to support the principles of chastity, the key idea is restraint in sexuality.[7] Meyer's goal for her organization is to move beyond therapeutic sexuality.

While this may be an extreme example of radical reverence for chastity's sacredness, nonetheless it is an effort to address a need, in nontheological terms, for sex in the context of a life-long, loving marital commitment. *Chaste* derives from the Latin root for "pure." In our culture, reverence for marriage to the extent that one is irrevocably committed to sexual purity within the confines of heterosexual marriage requires enormous resolve.

One senses painful skepticism about relationships and sex among the membership of the National Chastity Association. But in the not-too-distant theological past of Protestant Christians, celibacy and chastity were considered sacred gifts that one gives either to the church as a priest or nun or to the holy sacrament of marriage. The NCA, in its defiance of a cultural libertarian sexuality, struggles through a secular means to reclaim the special gift of sex in the marriage relationship. The Meyer group does not believe that equal, exclusive, faithful, lasting romantic love actually exists. Perhaps the NCA's obsession with chastity is taking the sacredness of sex too far for most people, but its purpose reminds us of the need for restraint and respect in our sexual conduct.

**3.** *Toward a Morality of Sexuality.* Developing a positive sexual morality is difficult. Attaining a healthy sexual balance in life is very difficult. We are called to achieve positive sexual relationships that draw us out of the little prison of self-adoring and self-satisfying sexuality into what C. S. Lewis calls the "oppositional delight" of another sexual being. We are also called to the moral restraint expressed in the valuing of chastity and celibacy that saves and honors our sexuality for *the one* most special to us in marriage or in spiritual service in the church.

In sexual matters as in all of our Christian life, we are called to walk by faith. That means that we don't have to have all the answers on our own ahead of time. That would not be trusting God to lead and offer grace in our sexuality as well as in other areas of life. It may be wise to recall the gracious invitation of 2 Chronicles 20:15 when the Lord says, "The battle is not yours but God's." We don't have to fight all the battles. We need to realize that God cares for us. God has given us sexuality and, if we trust God to give God the glory, God will be responsible for us and to us.

## CONCLUSION

Truly, we are sexual beings created in the image of God. God is God, and God is also a sexual being. We are called to enjoy our sexuality, to glorify God in our sexuality, and to believe that God participates in what God has created. At the same time, we are not given license to indulge ourselves in therapeutic sexuality. Sexuality is good, but there are restraints.

Little in this chapter has been written directly about homosexuality. This silence is for a theological reason: we begin with God, not our sexual experience. We need to establish theological priorities. Discussion about sexuality and homosexuality begins with God, not with us. In chapter 2, the purpose and intention of our created sexuality are addressed.

# The Purpose of Sexuality Is Intimacy

S exuality and intimacy go together. *Sexuality* is a more comprehensive and expansive term than *sex,* which traditionally is identified with biologically derived sexual impulses associated primarily with genital sexuality. By contrast, sexuality permeates each aspect of life. *Intimacy* is more than overt sexual behavior. Intimacy has its focus on the quality of one's relationship with body, feelings, sense of self, and interpersonal relationships, including those with God, the church, Jesus, and the Holy Spirit.

We are sexual beings, but that status does *not* guarantee satisfying sexuality or automatically create intimate interpersonal or spiritual relations. Each of us has the potential for satisfying sexual and intimate relationships. Intimacy is essentially relational. It moves beyond one's status as male, female, married, unmarried, single, or single again. In fact, Paul's expression of the deepest intimacy in human experience transcends the status advantage that may be perceived between male and female, Greek and Jew, slave and free. Human distinctions of holy and unholy are blurred in the unifying, spiritual nature of intimacy. Intimacy does not deny the sex act nor does it erase one's awareness of the sexuality of being male or female. True intimacy gathers up both sex and sexuality and integrates them into a higher order of relationship and sensitivity. This aspect of sexuality is the focal point of this chapter.

## Sex and God

As sexual beings we are invited to engage in sexual behavior at three levels. The purpose of each level, theologically speaking, is to enhance human life and our relationship with God. The first level is the highest and most complex; it is spiritual *intimacy*. The second level is *recreational* sexuality. The third level is biological *procreation*—keeping the species going. We explore these three levels in more detail.

**1.** *Intimacy—Breath of Life.* The distinguishing hallmark of human life is symbolized in the creation narratives of Genesis 1 and 2. In Genesis 2:7 the Lord formed man (human beings) of dust from the ground, breathed into his nostrils the *breath of life,* and man became a living being. The spiritually distinguishing characteristic of human beings is the intimacy with God imparted by that breath of life. The breath of life is God's supreme gift of intimacy to us. God invites us to enjoy and engage God at this deepest level of intimacy, which includes the sexual aspects of our humanity. Likewise, as human beings we are to breathe the breath of life into the gardens of Eden of our lives: work, children, spouse, church involvement—whatever may be the garden of life for us. To inspire another is the highest level of intimacy and the most profound expression of human sexuality.

**2.** *Recreation—Fellowship.* We are created to enjoy our sexuality. God delightfully intends for us, as sexual human beings, to enjoy recreational sexuality. Human sexuality and the stimulating responses and fulfillment of sexual behavior are ours to enjoy. God gives this aspect of our sexuality to us for our enjoyment. Playful or recreational sexuality should not be confused with the breath of life that distinguishes human beings (Genesis 2:7) from the rest of creation.

Some Christians have difficulty with recreational sexuality. They believe intimacy must be spiritualized. That belief denies sexual feelings and behaviors or suppresses them for the believer who seeks spiritual intimacy but fears social and sexual intimacy. We may readily appreciate the procreational value of sex. But some, for theological reasons, want to limit sexual behavior to biological, not enjoyable, purposes. This second level of human sexuality is what we might call recreational or in more theological terms relational sex. It is the most difficult aspect of sexuality to receive as God's gift. God calls us to intimacy with each other but in a *committed* relationship. We learn about each other through the other's body and emotions and are invited to enjoy each other through body and emotions, not just words and deeds. Relational sex is *playing together,* yes! But as God's gift and invitation, it is to occur in a committed relationship. Recreational sex for the Christian is a higher calling than finding a sexual playmate who is eager simply to learn the rules of a sexual "tennis game" but remains uninterested or unwilling to make a relational commitment.

Relational sex does not call us directly into intimate spiritual conversation with God, nor does it call us to procreation of the species.

**3.** *Procreation—Keep the Species Going.* A more traditional and simplistic theological view of sex restricts its purpose to procreational events; that is, sexual intercourse is to produce offspring. Those holding this view consider intercourse without expressed intention of propagating the species to be a theological error. This view eliminates recreational sex and creates a wide chasm between the sexuality identified with intercourse and the subtle forms of sexuality seen in the intimacy of our close walk with God. The tradition that places the greatest emphasis on procreational sex has its sexual priorities in reverse order. Procreation is necessary. But preservation of the species is not the primary purpose for which human beings have sex.

In summary, the highest form and purpose of sexuality is the intimacy implied in the unique relationship of God with Adam and Eve in Genesis 2. The gift of the "breath of life" includes both spiritual and sexual aspects. The second level of intimacy and sexuality is recreational sex. The third purpose of our sexuality is procreation. We are biological beings, but we are more

than purely instinctual creatures. The species must continue and
will. God will provide. The uniquely human function of sexuality, however, is to engage in relational sex; and, at a more
refined level, to experience the sexual intimacy of inhaling
deeply the "breath of life" with God.

## Sex and the Natural Order

**1.** *Natural Order Is Not Determinative.* Most traditional
Christian theology grants a high priority to the natural order or
natural law. This theological perspective assumes that God is
God and Creator and that within the created laws of the universe there is a moral purpose. There is a natural resolve
designed to glorify God and this shall not be violated. This theological position was dominant during the so-called Dark Ages
when nature seemed to overwhelm the human spirit by its vicis-
situdes, chaos, and uncontrollability. It was a courageous con-
fession of faith to believe that a natural order or a natural law
exists *under* God's divine providence.

Today's world view is a product of the Enlightenment.
Renaissance theology considered the natural order little more
than signposts or mile markers of God's providence. Human
life may have certain limits set by biological mechanisms and
social cohesiveness, but "modern man" has come to believe
that although the natural order or natural law may exist and
influence the human spirit, it does not contain the human spirit
or limit its imagination and vision of a more humane future.

For theological reasons I agree with the criticism of Sigmund
Freud's belief that the body is destiny. Body is *not* destiny. Biological mechanisms do not determine how human life is lived
or the *purpose* of sexuality or play. Humans are not disembodied spirits. We are called to an integration of body and spirit.
The body does *not* determine personality or sexuality.

To make the theological claim that heterosexuality is normative includes an assumption that biological and sociological

factors are less significant in determining sexual orientation than is the intention of God in creating humans as male and female to engage in heterosexual behavior. A strict determinist would argue that heterosexuality or homosexuality is predetermined by God and would include in that argument homosexual behavior, fantasies, or longings. This reasoning leads to an essentialist position that we are created either homosexual or heterosexual.[1] It may be more accurate theologically to claim that homosexuals are heterosexuals engaging in homosexual longings, fantasies, and acts. The so-called "unnatural behavior" of Romans 1 refers to an unnaturalness or distortion of sexuality that occurs outside the intention of God. Paul declares that sexuality is God's gift to us. One implication of Paul's assertions in Romans 1 is that heterosexuals and homosexuals have in common their "natural creation" as heterosexuals. It is the practice of giving oneself over to homosexual or "unnatural acts" that constitutes the theological and behavioral problems.

A naive appeal to natural theology elevates the procreational dimension of sexuality above other forms of sexuality and creates theological division between homosexuals and heterosexuals. On the other side of the theological argument is the elevation of recreational sex above other forms, which prompts the homosexual community to dismiss heterosexuals who engage in procreational sex as "breeders" who maintain that their sex acts are of a higher purpose. This misuse of arguments from natural theology gives rise to the charge and countercharge of homophobia and heterophobia.

We humans are sexual beings created by God with a purpose of enjoying our sexuality. The Scriptures, especially Genesis 1–3, bear clear witness to the purpose of sexual intercourse: it is to be heterosexual. Individuals who fantasize about or engage in homosexual acts, from a theological perspective, engage in activities that do not differ in *kind* from heterosexual actions, only *degree*. If they differed in kind, we would have two different *kinds* or *sets* of sexual acts, one for homosexuals and one for heterosexuals.

What establishes homosexuals and heterosexuals as of "like kind" is, first, both are created by the same God and in God's image. Second, in participating in sexual intercourse both may seek either to meet recreational or intimacy needs. Heterosexuals may also engage in sexual intercourse for procreational reasons. All homosexual acts, however, seek only recreational or intimacy needs. In this case homosexual persons express similar sexual enjoyment preferences as heterosexuals living out the "sexual revolution." Both place the emphasis on fun, feeling good, and feeling close to someone. Procreation sometimes occurs for the heterosexual, but it frequently is considered an "accident of biology." The limited purpose and content of the sexual relationship in this situation are the same as in homosexuality. From a traditional theological position, one could offer the argument that where sexual activity is limited to recreational or intimacy needs and not open to procreational sex, both heterosexuals and homosexuals engage in the same kind of sin.

In addition to the theological arguments that both homosexuals and heterosexuals share the same *kind* of creation and differ in sexual activity only in *degree,* psychological researchers on homosexuality have concluded that the differences are developmental and experiential and do not result from different kinds of human beings.[2]

**2.** *Object Choice Is Not Innate.* Psychiatrist Charles W. Socarides, a professor at the Albert Einstein College of Medicine, a collaborating psychoanalyst at the Columbia Institute and author of more than forty professional papers and two books on homosexuality, writes, "The claim that homosexuality is simply a variant of normal sexual behavior and exists alongside heterosexuality as an *equivalent expression of adult sexual maturation is utterly false."* Dr. Socardies amplifies his conclusion from clinical research, citing four basic behaviors. First we note his claim: "Homosexual object choice is not innate or instinctual, nor is heterosexual object choice, since both are learned behavior." Second, Socardies expands his clinical conclusion: "Only massive childhood fears can damage and disrupt the standard male-female pattern. Such early unconscious fears are responsible for the later development of homosexuality."[3]

Object relations theory is simply another effort to say that we are not predetermined either by body or a natural order in choice of object relations and love objects.[4] Socardies and other object-relations theorists argue, from clinical experience, that object relation choices are learned from early childhood. People learn a preference for specific forms of stimulation and seek specific modes of affection. Some of these choices may be constructive, others destructive. As human beings, our choice of whom and what we love is movable, ambiguous, and ever-changing. We are not predetermined.

A theological restatement of this principle declares that we are saved by faith through grace, and that not of ourselves. The natural order does not save. The call to the Christian life is a lifelong theological vocation that requires steadfast discipline and constant attention to behavior, attitudes, and a desire to follow the way that God has revealed to us.

Our object choice is neutral or ambiguous, not predetermined. Both theological and sociological influences are instrumental in the choices made and feelings associated with those actions.

In summary, sex is neither blessed nor cursed by the natural order. Sex is one means for achieving intimacy. Humans are not disembodied spirits and not merely animals. Nor is our destiny determined by mind over matter. An active interaction exists between the natural order of body and sexual instinct—and the resolve and free will of the human spirit.

## Male and Female

Theological assumptions and discussion in Western Christian thought, especially for classical Roman Catholicism and Protestantism, proceed from categories that stress the divine self-sufficiency of God and the innate spiritual powerlessness of human beings. The emphasis upon God's transcendence and self-sufficiency coupled with human immanence and passive dependence upon the will of God has inadvertently created a theological dilemma that bears specific implications for a theology of sexuality. The power, transcendence, and impassionability of God are predictably associated with the idealized form of male social and sexual behavior. The logic that depicts God and men as the "Unmoved Movers" decrees that the Christian female is the corresponding opposite: powerless, immanent, passionate, and acting not through will but through the affections and feelings.

This theological paradigm of divine/human relations has become, perhaps unwittingly, the male/female paradigm for many Christians. An extension of this theological model will associate strength, wisdom, purity, and power with men and will ascribe weakness, emotionality, sin, and low self-esteem to women. Many contemporary Christian thinkers, especially the feminist theologians, have been critical of the resultant patriarchal theology and family structure in which "women of faith will end up in the doubly dependent role of subjugation to God and the male."[5]

**1.** *Masculinity.* The influence of a theological tradition that includes what Catherine Keller phrases as "The Embarrassment of God" places an emphasis upon at least three traditionally held and valued male traits. First, the male is the Unmoved Mover and remains externally related to women; it is after all a man's world. Second, women are perceived as the "second sex" (a term coined by Simone de Beauvoir), created inferior to men and doubly inferior to deity. They are to respond as to their work as "the soluble self, which dissolves into relation" with the man. Third, men are valued for their separateness, impassionability, power, and self-interest, not connectiveness, mutuality, and the giving of life rather than the *risking* of life in intimacy and love.[6]

James Nelson, a professor of theology at United Theological Seminary of the Twin Cities, has spent much of his career writing about the theology of sexuality. In a theological essay, "Men and Body Life," he observes that traditional wisdom reinforces a masculinity that does not encourage tenderness, intimacy, and mutuality and is a destructive force that leads to sexual abuse. From a theological perspective, Nelson claims that "masculinity is too largely a negative identity because it is grounded in body alienation." Because men tend to focus on the external, what's out there both spiritually and sexually, they remain at odds with the spirituality and mystery within their own being. Overcoming "body alienation" means receiving "their sexuality as internal, deep and mysterious" and becoming less governed by traditional imagery of sexuality and spirituality that is function-oriented, not mystery-oriented.[7]

**2.** *Femininity.* In the parallel categories of dominance, submission, and mutuality, conventional theological wisdom about women suggests the following. First, women are complex, highly experiential, emotional, and secretive; therefore, they need to come under the simple dominance of men. Second, by submitting their complexity and emotionality to the simple dominance of men, women can channel their mysterious complexity, guide their primary function of motherhood, and turn their energies toward their nurturing, mothering "nature" better than they themselves can do. A third assumption holds that mutuality, intimacy, and nurture are to be offered by women to please or build up men. Missing in the traditional theology of femininity is an admonition for women to learn to separate and develop self-transcendence.

**3.** *An Alternative.* A reexamination of traditional theological and scriptural interpretations suggests first that many of the traditional social and psychological assumptions are stereotypes of masculinity and femininity and need to be set straight. Second, we do not find categorical, fundamental differences between men and women. For example, when King David decided to commit adultery with Bathsheba (2 Samuel 11), his plan was every bit as complex an act of seduction as any contrived by a woman. Recall that King David had lusted after Bathsheba, the wife of Uriah, a general in David's army. David arranged for Uriah to spearhead a contingent of the Hebrew army into battle against the Ammorites "in the forefront of the hardest fighting" with instructions that the rest of the king's army should "then draw back from him, that he may be struck down, and die" (2 Samuel 11:15). This was David's devious sexual strategy without openly violating the law. Uriah would be out of the way so Bathsheba could be David's sex object.

To cover his sin of lust and murder, David arranged a military strategy that would assure Bathsheba's becoming a widow. Then the benevolent king befriended her. The sexual seduction and manipulation were all of the king's doing. There was no female intrigue in this episode of a biblical soap opera. David's wanton lust, not female seduction, was the cause of this sexual immorality.

Second, submitting to one another makes life more complicated, not less. Submission of any kind, whether unilateral or mutual, does not make life less complicated. If one subscribes to a *unilateral* submission as a result of being overpowered and having one's inner life suppressed, the consequent relation is laced with conflict, ambivalence, uncertainty, and insecurity. This would hardly present a picture of simple unitive satisfaction. If a *mutual* submission exists between two people, one based upon jointly encouraged and shared self-disclosures that are emotionally and intellectually well received by each other, life together is established upon tremendously complex sensitivities and understandings that are mutually derived.

Third, the goal for appropriate expression of maleness and femaleness is mutuality and intimacy. Dominance and submission are social or power categories; whereas Genesis 2 reminds us that God's gift of the "breath of life" to humanity is an invitation for us to enjoy a higher level of relationship and intimacy with God than that of any other creature. The scriptures invite us into a new understanding of the purpose of sexuality and intimacy in male-female relationships.

## Homosexuality: Caught in the Crossfire

**1.** *Innate, Instinctual, or Learned?* John McNeill is a Jesuit priest who has long advocated that homosexuals be given more theological and social status within the church. He declares homosexuality is not a pathology but a God-given gift.[8] Other theologians, especially Norman Pittenger and D. S. Bailey, support McNeill's position.[9] Father McNeill espouses an essentialist position influenced by natural law and natural theology: homosexuality is not learned; it is natural and a normal part of creation.[10] Homosexuality is innate and therefore, McNeill believes, God-given. Most homosexuals, especially males who identify themselves as Christians, would share Father McNeill's position.

On the other hand, the more traditional position interprets Genesis 1–3 to declare that heterosexual behavior is the intended expression of human sexuality. Homosexuality is seen as a variant of the norm. Some traditionalists perceive homosexuality as a function of inadequate childrearing practices such as parental withholding of positive affection. Other traditionalists would offer a harsher assessment: homosexuality is a perversion and must be treated as a psychological pathology. Others would argue that homosexuality is more than a biological or psychological problem; it is a spiritual problem. These positions refer to Romans 1 and 1 Corinthians 6 where Paul's statements appear to claim that homosexuality is a theological perversion more than a biological dysfunction.

A theological position that claims homosexuality is "God-given" must go beyond the argument advanced by Steven Reid that sexual orientation is socially determined. In his 1986 presentation to the United Methodist Commission on the Status and Role of Women, Reid argues that the Genesis references to man to be fruitful and multiply are limited to a rural, agrarian society. Therefore God's message to ancient Israel in Genesis 1:28 that survival and development of the nation depends upon being procreationally fruitful would have been essential for the survival of a primitive, agrarian culture. But alas, we live in a different world today where a definite call to advance the population rate is no longer a primary mission of God's people. In the ancient Israelite setting, one could, according to Reid, draw inferences from Genesis 1:28 that would be a basis for intolerance to homosexuality. In a modern, more urbane, sophisticated, and advanced culture where numerical survival is not a central theological concern, one would expect to find a tolerance, indeed a theological acceptance of homosexuality, if Reid's position is to be persuasive.[11]

Such an analysis may suggest some interesting sociological speculations about procreation, sensibilities, and psycho-social refinements, as well as offer some reflections on the value of civilizations continuing beyond a single generation. However that discussion may evolve, it exists quite apart from judging the theological adequacy of using Genesis 1:28 to assert that homosexuality is God-given for the twentieth century while not for early Israel. A principle of theological consistency would suggest that the theological basis for declaring heterosexuality as normative in Genesis *and* today is based finally not on sociology but theology.

**2.** *Open/Closed Affectionate Parents.* A number of studies have endeavored to suggest that several "parental factors in the childhood of homosexuals" are at work in the development of a homosexual orientation. Some have observed a positive correlation between "close-binding-intimate" mother with the father who is "detached, hostile, and in some other way unable to provide the son with a positive relationship." The suggestion is advanced that over-positive mothers, over-indulgent mothers, or over-permissive mothers along with negative, unavailable fathers are root causes of homosexual behavior.[12]

For each study that cites the socialization effects of early childhood experience and parent/child interaction, someone will speculate or may offer an exception to the study. Especially

painful and damaging to gay and lesbian persons are studies
that suggest that their lives are predetermined by early childhood experiences over which they had no control or that there
is a biological predetermination toward homosexuality. We all
have some residual problems that grow out of early childhood
experiences. They may be very powerful influences, and at
times these seem determinative and may lead us to despair over
the inescapability of our past. But change and healing are possible. That healing is not self-directed but occurs only in relationship in community. For the Christian, it is the power of Christ
as manifested in and witnessed through the community of
believers that is available, in Christian love, to help redirect the
power and weight of previous experience.

In the studies from psychology and psychiatry as well as the
sociological analyses of cultural forces, we find collaborative
evidence to support the appeal and promise of the gospel.
Regardless of our past and how we may perceive it or experience it, change is possible. There may be in effect a genetic predisposition for homosexuality just as there may be predispositions for all kinds of conditions: alcoholism, depression, cancer,
heart problems. Having a predisposition does not make the
resultant behavior or medical or emotional condition a good or
advisable one.

The suggestion of the theory regarding differences in open
and closed affectionate parents is that while the child has very
little control over the impact of early experience and may not
be able, as a result of developmental trauma, to maintain much
control over thoughts about homosexuality, there remains a
*very real difference between thoughts and actions.* The thoughts
and feelings may be seen as symbolic of the injury, disease, or
predisposition toward homosexuality. From a theological perspective, the thoughts and feelings are recognized as a symp-
tom of sin, not of homosexuality.

The theological problem in supporting social determinism is
the concession that an external or social force controls or abso-
lutely determines one's life on the basis of key environmental

factors, including, for example, parents. An example of radical social control is seen in George Orwell's novel *1984,* in which the problems deriving from "big brother's" absolute social control are frighteningly played out. A radical essentialist position would claim a person is born as a homosexual and nothing through experience, training, parental influence, or spiritual guidance would change that individual's homosexuality. In fact, the claim from this position is that homosexuality is God's gift and to try to live as a heterosexual is a denial of a God-given sexual orientation.

**3.** *Dominance and Submission.* Barbara Zanotti, in *Homosexuality in the Catholic Church,* claims that the traditional male dominance in society represents a cause-and-effect relationship between male dominance and hatred of women. She uses Mary Daly's phrase "When God is a male, the male is God" to make her case. In the family or society based on male dominance, women are not complementary to or companions of men but are valued as existing for men's pleasure; men's work, power and experience are all that really matter. Zanotti expands her argument to claim that male-dominated societies are a function of and derived from enforced heterosexuality, that wherever heterosexuality exists one has male dominance, oppression of women, and a destructive theology.[13]

When sexual behavior or sexual orientation is used to advance a theological position, one consequence is an exacerbation of theological dialogue. In this study, the theological conflict plunges gay men and lesbians into a crossfire between feminist theologians and traditional theologians. The church needs to develop that aspect of our theology that affirms the intimate, wooing, tender nature of God, without at the same time injecting any sexual orientation into the center of that controversy. We need to shift our understanding of our intimate, mystical relationship with God. As the argument stands now, the tender, sensitive side of God unfortunately has become a sexual argument not a theological affirmation.

**4.** *Sexual Stereotyping.* Sex roles are primarily social roles and are not related to sexual behavior. The increase of dual-career marriages, single-parent families, and women who have moved into jobs traditionally associated with men destroys many of the traditional sex-role stereotypes.

Americans still struggle over the possibility of a woman becoming vice-president or even president of the United States. In some countries women have been or were heads-of-state for years: Golda Meier, the queens of England, Margaret Thatcher, Corazon Aquino, Indira Gandhi, Benazir Bhutto. The United States needs to adjust its naive, traditional sex-role typologies to be more inclusive of women's capacities to lead and use power. Such a shift would affirm that both men and women, regardless of social and political roles, remain sexual beings who can enjoy both social and sexual intimacy.

Gay men are often characterized as weak and passive, lesbians as mannish or "butch." These are insensitive and inappropriate characterizations of a homosexual lifestyle or sexual expression. As James Harrison put it, "In short, the one thing homosexual people have in common other than their sexual orientation is not a standard behavior pattern, a predictable kind of talent, a particular measure of virtue or any other human characteristic; it is, rather, a common experience of discrimination. It is because of intolerance that so many are invisible and it is largely because of invisibility that stereotypes persist."[14]

**5.** *Fears of Opposite Sex.* Mental health researcher Luise J. Zucker believes, along with Sandor Rado, that homosexuality may be less an overt attraction to the same sex and more the "incapacitating fears of the opposite sex." Zucker found that focusing on homosexuals' "relations with people, regardless of sex" proved very fruitful.[15]

Others, like William G. Herron, consider the problem of "inadequate mothering" and the difficulty in developing a "capacity to deal with anxiety related to being separated from one's parents" as significant explanatory categories regarding the difficulty among gay men in developing long-term, satisfying intimate relations. The anxiety and conflict about one's identity and sexuality eventuates "in the avoidance of bonds with steady partners, though the desire for a close relationship remains."[16]

The dilemma of how one is attracted to people of the same sex and/or fearful of positive bonds with someone of the opposite sex remains a difficult question for both theologians and psychologists. Some would argue that behavior based on such attraction is theological rebellion; some would claim that it is arrested psychological development; others would maintain that it is a natural attraction or that such feelings and behaviors of attraction are in-born. While the debate rages on, those with homosexual attractions live with the pain brought on by the difficulty of experiencing genuine intimate and sustained human relations within the gay or lesbian community. The pain is further compounded by the fact that gays and lesbians find little positive support from those who live outside the homophile community. The conflict is very real for both heterosexuals and homosexuals who struggle to better understand themselves in the light of those who do not share their sexual orientation.


## CONCLUSION

Intimacy is the high road of human life. In the words of Paul Lehmann, God's purpose for us is "to make and to keep human life human."[17] That's an equally compelling invitation and perplexing problem for all human beings, regardless of sexual orientation.

The key function of human sexuality is *not* procreation or even recreation. But it is to move us toward higher levels of intimacy with one another and with God. While all of our conduct is in some way sexual behavior, the goal for the Christian life is to place our sexuality in the larger context of mutuality, intimacy (spiritual, emotional, and sexual) that draws us toward greater wholeness and does not relegate sexual behavior to strictly physical acts. Much stereotyping of sexual behavior and sex roles has been handed down through a biased philosophical system and a misunderstanding of God's intention for creation.

We are created as male and female, separate and distinct but as equals. We must confess our sins of misinterpretation of the role of men and women across the years, in which men have been guaranteed or been required to live out roles of dominance, while women have been forced into roles of submission. In Christ we are equals and need to begin to exercise the freedom we have in the gospel to become peers with one another as male and female.

One of the theological and psychological themes of this study is my belief that *the development of homosexuality can be laid at the feet of a culture and a church that "requires" men to be externally organized and women to do all the nurturing.* This abuse and misrepresentation of the gospel in part contributes to the conflicts and inadequacies of parental influences in childhood development that lead to homosexuality.

As men and women are being called to reassess their sexuality and their sexual and social roles, the newly found freedoms are both invigorating and frightening. They inspire, because we are called to a higher level of mutuality and trust. They create immense risk, because we can use the freedoms to justify anything we want to do sexually.

How we express our sexuality and how we find satisfaction and intimacy are, in many ways, influenced by those with whom we have had close contact. Our sexuality may be positive, warm, close, and intimate; or, it may be rejecting, cajoling, over-protective, over-indulgent, or overly permissive. If we do not encourage others by our behavior to make their lives more human, then we have failed in our Christian calling. If we are not encouraged by others' Christian behavior to make our lives more human, then we have failed in our Christian response.

# CHAPTER 3

# Heterosexual and Homosexual Lifestyles

## Introduction

C reation is to glorify God both in how we live and in our relationship to God.[1]

In the creation narratives of Genesis 1–3, the assumption of heterosexuality is clear. Heterosexuality is normative for men and women as God-created beings. In the Genesis account of creation, heterosexuality is the standard expectation for human behavior and conduct.

## Paradigm of the Family of God

**1.** *Husband and Wife (Adam and Eve).* Three qualities about the "original" husband and wife form a paradigm for relations between the sexes.

*a) Together.* In Genesis 2:20 we read, "but for the man there was not found a helper as his partner." The text suggests that none of the beasts of the field, nor birds of the air nor other living creatures were peers of Adam. The biblical account declares that God first caused a deep sleep to fall upon Adam and then created woman (Genesis 2:21-23). The companionship, mutuality, and camaraderie that God proposes for human beings cannot be supplied by any means other than the man-woman or male-female relation. The initial problem of loneliness was resolved at the beginning by God's creating male and female to provide the most intimate and supportive of human relations.

*b) Equality.* Some Bible students declare that Eve is identified with the rib of Adam and point to Adam's words, "This at
last is bone of my bones and flesh of my flesh" (Genesis 2:23),
and infer that women are created inferior to or lower than men.
The context of the passage, however, makes it clear that God
did not want an inferior helper. The equality of male and
female, Adam and Eve, is clear. In fact, one might argue, as
some commentators have, that woman is the crowning act of
creation. Certainly she is not an inferior helpmate (Genesis
2:23-24). The equality of father and mother is matched by the
parallelism of the young man who leaves his parents, marries a
wife as an equal, and they become one flesh (Genesis 2:24).
The term "one flesh" indicates a unity and an equality. If
inequality were to be implied among men and women in the
family of God, images like "Adam and his companion" or
"Adam and his helper" would have been used.

Further, the concept of equality of male and female receives
a helpful interpretation by Paul Jewett. He argues that in Jesus'
relationship to women in the New Testament, the principle of
equality in the Gospel begins to surface. While none of the
original disciples was female, Jesus' acceptance of women is
evident: look, for example, at his treatment of his mother, Mary
Magdalene, the Samaritan woman at Jacob's Well, Mary and
Martha, Mary the mother of James the Less and of Joses and
Salome. In each of these relationships we see Jesus extending
the paradigm of the family of God to bring about equality
between men and women, males and females.[2]

*c) Extend/Build the Kingdom.* The Genesis 1 creation account
uses a more formal and less poetic style than does chapter 2. In
Genesis 1:27-28, the family relation between God and human
beings is established as one of similarity. Likewise, equality of
male and female is clearly established. God blesses this intimate equality, "Be fruitful and multiply, and fill the earth and
subdue it" (1:28). The paradigm or pattern clearly is a heterosexual one that follows immediately after creation of female-

ness and maleness. The notion of being fruitful and multiplying is, of course, not limited simply to the numbers of people that are created through sexual intercourse. But the paradigm extends to the heterosexual family in which children are conceived, raised, and nurtured into maturity. Heterosexuality is the paradigm for the family of God.

**2.** *Exceptions for the Kingdom.* In both the Old and New Testaments and throughout church history not everyone has married. The model of heterosexual families also has positive exceptions.

*a) Celibacy.* In taking a vow of celibacy, one pledges that the gift of sexuality will be set aside for the purpose of building up the Kingdom. To be celibate does not mean one has no sex drive or fears sex. Rather celibacy is a sacrifice of one's sexual energy and human commitment that is offered lovingly to God. "Be fruitful and multiply" takes on a more spiritual and less procreational embodiment.

Many Protestants hold a false idea about celibacy—that it is a running away from sexuality rather than a gift of one's sexuality to the larger family of God. Protestants would be well served to put their theology of celibacy on a more positive, normative theological plane.

*b) Not Giving or Being Given in Marriage.* Paul was so convinced of the immediacy of the coming of the Kingdom, the urgency of the hour, and the heavy demands of building and extending the Kingdom that he advocated exempting oneself from marriage for the sake of the church. In 1 Corinthians 7:25-31, Paul makes it clear that this exception to the paradigm is not a "command of the Lord" but his own personal preference. Perhaps from painful personal experience, he admonishes believers, "Yet those who marry will have worldly troubles, and I would spare you that." The apostle wants simply to press on with all energy to build the Kingdom. "The unmarried man is anxious about the affairs of the Lord, how to please the Lord" (1 Corinthians 7:32). Understanding that the paradigm for the family of God is heterosexual marriage, Paul makes it clear that his preference for a theological exception is due to the urgency of the hour in the life of the Kingdom. It is a theological not a sexual reason for celibacy.

## Types of Intimacy

**1.** *Spiritual Intimacy.* In the previous chapter, I argued that the highest level of intimacy is spiritual intimacy with God. In the New Testament setting, this intimacy is offered to us in the incarnation of Jesus. The intimacy and unity of the church are possible only through the coming of the Holy Spirit, who continues the work of Christ.

Whether male or female, married or unmarried, celibate or sexually active, the highest form of intimacy is spiritual intimacy with God.

**2.** *Friendship Intimacy.* Deep human friendships exist between men and between women, and *philia* relations exist between unmarried men and unmarried women. Friendship intimacy affords a level of connectedness that goes deeper and is more powerful than the physical intimacy of sexual intercourse. For example, the friendship of David and Jonathan was a powerful and lasting friendship. It achieved a level of friendship and intimacy not duplicated in any sexual intimacy that David or Jonathan might have had with women.

This is not to say that friendship was a homosexual relationship, although some writers have made that claim. In his study *Jonathan Loved David,* Tom Horner asserts:

> There can be little doubt, however, except on the part of those who absolutely refuse to believe it, that there existed a homosexual relationship between David and Jonathan.

Horner believes that passages from 1 Samuel 18:1 and 2 Samuel 1:26 make transparent the homosexual love of Jonathan for

David and vice versa. This love cannot be dismissed as a metaphor for *philia* affection. Using research gained from study of other ancient Eastern and Near Eastern cultures, Horner observes three common types of homosexual practice: "noble lovers, catamites, and plain average citizens." Locating the relationship of Jonathan and David with the practice of nobility, Horner concludes:

> David was not a "homosexual" because he loved Jonathan, or Jonathan because he loved David. They were simply well-rounded men who acted fully within the standards of a society that had been dominated for two hundred years by an Aegean culture—a culture that accepted homosexuality.[3]

Horner also makes the claim that a similar same-sex bond probably existed between Ruth and Naomi, and between Jesus and his disciples.[4] While the influences of neighboring cultures are reflected in aspects of Israelite society, Horner's pivotal point rests on data gathered from pagan cultures of the period and extends the sociology and history of these people to apply directly—from an argument of scriptural silence—to Israelite sexual practices, especially among nobility. Israel may have been similar to the other nations in some regards, but Israelite insistence on heterosexuality is one of the ways in which it was *dissimilar* to the Greek and Aegean peoples.

In the intimacy of the Jonathan-and-David relationship, we find the closeness both of a personal attraction and also the closeness that often forms between people of very different and unlikely personalities who go through crises together. The crises of war and combat, of pain, or of natural disaster form friendship bonds that endure through a lifetime and are power-fully intimate. The close bonding formed by teammates on same-sex teams in swimming, football, gymnastics, cycling, field and track, are not likely to be duplicated in other contexts or perhaps even with marriage partners. The intimacy of this type of relationship is neither exclusively spiritual nor sexual. It is the integration toward wholeness of *epithymia, philia, eros,* and *agape*. A balanced expression of the four dimensions of love makes for enduring human friendship and affection.

Jesus' close relationship with Mary Magdalene and his mother is quite normal. The New Testament gives no indication of any neurotic or incestuous activity between Jesus' mother and himself. Likewise, Jesus' close friendship with Mary Magdalene was a bond that gave her the strength and the courage to remain at the foot of the cross to grieve for all of us over the suffering of her Lord. Mary's intimate friendship empowered her to lead the group of other women to the tomb on Easter Sunday (Luke 24:1-3, 10, 11). The Scriptures do not play down the intimacy of David and Jonathan, nor that of Jesus and his male disciples or his female followers. Biblical writers understood that within the context of heterosexual paradigms, friendship intimacy does not violate heterosexual norms or commandments against adultery or incest.

**3.** *Sexual Intimacy.* Whether one considers the relationship in Adam and Eve's conception of Cain and Abel or Abraham and Sarah's conception of Isaac, the paradigm of sexual intimacy is that of sexual intercourse in a heterosexual relationship. The paradigm of the family of God assumes a heterosexual relationship as normative, and discussion of sexual intimacy in the Bible is offered in that light.

## Metaphors and Images for the Family of God

Beyond passages relating to husband and wife, male and female, a number of images or metaphors are used in the Bible that encourage as well as define areas of growth in faith.

**1.** *Bride/Bridegroom.* This image refers primarily to the relationship of the people of Israel with God (especially Isaiah 49:18; 61:10; 62:5; and also Jeremiah 2:2, 32; 7:34; 25:10). In the New Testament the most prevalent use of this imagery is found in Revelation and refers to the church as the bridegroom waiting for the coming of Jesus (Revelation 18:23; 19:7; 21:2, 9; 22:17). In Ephesians 5, the author compares the marriage relationship to Christ's relation to the church.

In the parable of the wise and foolish virgins (Matthew 25:1, 5-6, 10), the images clearly suggest that the heterosexuality of the bride and the bridegroom is to be duplicated in the family of God.

**2.** *Fidelity.* The seventh commandment, "You shall not commit adultery" (Exodus 20:14), assumes heterosexual relations. Images that relate to spiritual fidelity, faithfulness, and trusting belief all reflect a paradigm of heterosexuality. Language about prostitution and unfaithfulness in the Old Testament pertains to the violation of the fidelity and trust in a heterosexual marriage. Language that refers to nonheterosexual behavior is couched in terms such as "unnatural" (Romans 1:26).

**3.** *Sexuality.* The highly sensuous language of the Song of Solomon and some of the Proverbs endeavors to convey the depth of "spiritual intimacy." Some of the sexual imagery in the Song of Solomon is so graphic that it could be read as quasipornographic. However vivid and sensuous may be the images in the Wisdom Literature, they depict the sensuality and intimacy of heterosexuality. The sexual paradigm and poetic imagery used in the biblical narratives to express closeness to God are consistently heterosexual.

**4.** *Beloved.* At the time of Jesus' baptism, we are told, a voice from Heaven (God) affirms "my beloved Son" (Matthew 3:17; Mark 1:11; Luke 3:22). "Beloved" is used in both Old and New Testaments to convey spiritual intimacy and friendship intimacy: between God and Israel (Deuteronomy 33:12); between David and Jonathan (2 Samuel 1:23); in John's address to the church and to Gaius (1 John 2:7; 3:2, 21; 3 John 1:1, 2, 5, 11); and in the pastoral letters of Paul (Romans 1:7; 1 Corinthians 4:17; 15:58 and especially 2 Corinthians 12:19).

Numerous references in Psalms and the Song of Solomon

refer to the intimate, sensuous, and loving relationship between God and the faithful follower.

To summarize, the various sensuous, sexual, familial, and interpersonal images relating to the family of God in the Bible are based on a paradigm of heterosexuality.

## CONCLUSION

The claim of this chapter is that the consistent witness of Scripture attests to a paradigm of heterosexuality clearly evident in the creation narratives of Adam and Eve in Genesis as well as in numerous other passages that endeavor to express the intimacy of God's people. The positive images about human relations—husband and wife, male and female, parent and child—and the metaphors used to draw attention to the nurturing power of God and the Holy Spirit within the life of the church employ heterosexual language. Wherever sexual intimacy is discussed or analogies or metaphors are employed, the paradigms and safeguards assume heterosexuality as normative.

Little is said directly in the Bible about homosexuality, but where those passages occur in both Old and New Testaments, they are clear in their theological assumption that heterosexuality is the foundation of sexuality.

*PART II*


# A BIBLICAL
# PERSPECTIVE

# CHAPTER 4

# The Old Testament and Homosexuality

## Introduction

A detailed exploration of Old and New Testament texts on homosexuality requires several assumptions and ground rules.

First, in chapter 1 we discussed the assumption that human beings are sexual beings and that our sexuality is a gift from God in the act of creation itself. In chapter 2, we attempted to show the interrelationship of spiritual, emotional, and social intimacy and the integrative relationship in which Christian love pulls *epithymia, eros, philia,* and *agape* into a single wholeness in a mature Christian experience. In chapter 3 we maintained that heterosexuality is the assumed normative sexual category in biblical narratives and poetic imagery about God's relationship to humanity.

Part I (chapters 1–3) needs to be placed in the context of the Bible passages on homosexuality. Genesis 1–3 is the foundation for understanding God and humanity. Neither maleness alone nor femaleness alone reflects God's general intention for creation or God's character as revealed and expressed in creation.[1] Both Old and New Testaments share an assumption that heterosexuality is theologically normative.

Second, a word about words. The words *homosexual, gay,* and *lesbian* do not occur in Scripture. Language scholars report that the words *homosexual* and *homosexuality* were not in the

Hebrew or Greek vocabulary; and in fact, the *Oxford English Dictionary* states only that the noun *homosexual* was in use before 1897.[2] The King James Version (1611) does not use the term *homosexual* or its derivatives. First used in the *Revised Standard Version* (1946, 1953), and followed quickly by other English versions such as *The Living Bible* (1971) and the *New American Standard Version* (1988), the word *homosexual* is given interchangeable credence with "sexual perverts" and "homosexual perverts." In the light of this language background in the modern Bible versions, one can understand why the controversy over the Bible and homosexuality has become such a hotly contested and debated topic in recent years.

The words *sodomy* and *sodomite* are coined as derivatives from the ancient city of Sodom. The word *abomination* traditionally has been used in Scripture, with its basis in the Levitical Code, as reference to homosexual activities.

The infinitive *to know* traditionally has been understood as a euphemism for sexual intercourse. In our modern vernacular the idea of knowing or of having "carnal knowledge" is suggested by the 1971 movie title *Carnal Knowledge*, a specific reference to sexual intercourse.

Third, a word about the presentation of the interpretation of the biblical texts. Each passage will be examined from a threefold approach: the *traditional* interpretation, followed by the *revisionist* interpretation, and concluded with a third, *discussion*, section on the conflicts between the traditional and revisionist positions.

We begin with the traditional to set the background for the contemporary discussion and to inform the reader of the dominant historical interpretations of these key Bible passages. In the section on the revisionist interpretation, the reader needs to understand the approach and the logic used by those who challenge the traditional interpretation of the passages in which the issue of homosexuality is central. Finally, a discussion section will endeavor to suggest to the reader how the issues may be joined for discussion and the kinds of theological, pastoral, and emotional concerns that remain unanswered or unsettled in the current debate between traditional and the revisionist positions.

## Sodom and Gomorrah: Genesis 18:16–19:29

The context of the Sodom and Gomorrah story must be seen within the larger framework of God's challenge and promise in Genesis 11:28 and Genesis 12 where God makes the promise to Abram: "I will bless those who bless you, and the one who curses you I will curse; and in you all the families of the earth shall be blessed" (Genesis 12:3). As Abram and his family advanced from Ur of the Chaldeans to Canaan, Lot chose to locate in Sodom. Abram sought out other territory to claim (Genesis 13:12-13). When Lot occupied Sodom, its reputation for evil was well established. Because Sodom and Gomorrah were evil places, God reveals to Abraham a desire to destroy these cities (18:17, 19). On two occasions Abraham intercedes for the righteous (including Lot) who live within the city and successfully diverts God's initial plan.

Finally in chapter 19, God sends two angels or messengers to Sodom. They go to determine if the city is actually as wicked as the general outcry suggests. Their task is to prepare a "scouting report" for God, regarding any righteous persons and whether they are worth saving.

**1.** *Traditional Interpretation.* In Genesis 19, the storyline is fairly simple. Abraham's nephew, Lot, who has settled in Sodom receives the angelic visitors and extends a congenial, hospitable invitation to dinner. However, trouble is brewing. By nightfall all the males of Sodom gather outside Lot's house, demanding that the male messengers be sent out to them that they might "know" (i.e., have sexual intercourse with or carnal knowledge of) them. Lot refuses and instead offers his two daughters, who are promptly refused by the males of Sodom.

The males, now angered by Lot's refusal, break into Lot's

home in order to forceably "know" the male visitors. At the last minute the messengers intervene, striking the Sodomite males blind. The Lord's "pre-trial" inquiry into Sodom's degree of sinfulness is now concluded with *prima facie* evidence that the evil is worse than Abram might have imagined. The specific sin at the dinner hour is not Lot's inhospitality toward Sodomites casually dropping by the house to visit with God's messengers. Nor is the sin the Sodomites' inhospitality to the male angels. Rather the great evil that merits destruction of the city is the intended sin of homosexual rape.

For its general evil and the intention of homosexual rape, the Lord determines (19:13) to destroy the city and all its inhabitants, and does (19:24-28). The events of this episode or pericope bear testimony to God's holy wrath against the iniquity of Sodom's sin and its failure to entertain the holiness of God. Adding theological insult to theological injury, the Sodomites compounded their evil ways by attempting male homosexual rape with God's messengers of peace and mercy.

**2.** *Revisionist Interpretation.* D. S. Bailey in 1955[3] and John McNeill in 1976[4] are influential voices in revisionist reading of Genesis 18 and 19. Bailey's argument pivots on his claim that "get acquainted with" is actually the common-sense meaning of "to know." Bailey declares, "the demand to 'know' the visitors whom Lot had entertained may well have implied some serious breach of the rules of hospitality." Bailey's rationale is a statistical profile of the Hebrew verb *yādha'*, "to know." "To know" is used 943 times in the Old Testament, but in only ten cases does the term denote sexual intercourse. And then it is restricted to heterosexual acts.[5]

Old Testament references to Sodom (Jeremiah 23:14; Ezekiel 16:49-50), Bailey points out, never identify the sin of Sodom and Gomorrah as homosexuality. The sins of adultery, lying, an unrepentant heart, greed, prosperous self-centeredness, are the sins that merit destruction of the city. Further, concludes Bailey, not until Hellenistic or Greek influences penetrate Jewish thought in the later New Testament books (e.g., 2 Peter and Jude), do we find an explicit connection between Sodom and homosexual practices.[6] Robert Treese, in *Loving Women, Loving Men,* ponders the Bailey argument and concludes that whether "Bailey's conclusions will, in time, gain widespread acceptance is somewhat problematical."[7]

Likewise, Henri J. M. Nouwen, in *Intimacy,* chapter 3, "Homosexuality: Prejudice or Mental Illness?" declares that the story of Sodom and Gomorrah "does not condemn the homosexual act as a perversion but as a sin against the biblical virtue of hospitality. The people of Sodom misused visiting strangers, who were considered as special messengers of God."[8]

**3.** *Discussion.* The traditional interpretation claims that the destruction of Sodom and Gomorrah is punishment for the general sinfulness of the city. Homosexuality had become so rampant that Lot's refusal to give up God's messengers to male homosexual rape would be considered by the Sodomites a consummate act of inhospitality. The revisionist position maintains that *yādha'* refers to intellectual and social knowledge, not sexual intercourse. The sin can only be a breach of social hospitality—nothing more, nothing less.

In his discussion of this text, Victor Furnish sides with the traditionalists. His comments on the silence in Old Testament texts about homosexual language or acts are helpful. Heterosexuality was normative and "to know" meant sexual intercourse, and that goes without saying. Furnish observes that the influence of the Greek world and therefore the so-called Hellenization of Judaism developed across the centuries. Therefore by the end of the New Testament, it could go without saying that "to know" refers to sexual intercourse. Certainly by the Middle Ages the use of Sodomitic symbolism had been expanded to include and interpret activities and sins that covered everything from homosexual intercourse to male cult prostitution. One is cautioned by Furnish against making too direct a translation of sodomy and Sodomites to refer solely to homosexuality.[9]

## The Rape at Gibeah: Judges 19:22-25

**1.** *Traditional Interpretation.* Old Testament scholars see a parallel between the story of Lot and Sodom and the episode of the Levite and his concubine at Gibeah. The storyline, again, is fairly simple. The Levite was living in the country of Ephraim with his concubine (Judges 19:1). They had a fight. She went to Bethlehem to her people. Four months later the Levite travels from Ephraim to Bethlehem and eventually persuades her to return with him. They begin a trip north to Ephraim. The prospect of spending a night at Jebus (Jerusalem) was unsatisfactory because it was held by the Jebusites. The Levite and his concubine press on to "safe territory," Gibeah. Arriving late and finding no place available, the two plan to spend the night in the village square. An old man comes along and offers them his place to bed down for the night.

Now the drama begins (19:22-26). While the old man is engaged in "making their hearts merry" at his dinner table, "vile men" besiege the house, demanding the old man "bring out the man who came to your house that we may know him." The host refuses and castigates the ravenous mob. In an effort to placate them, he offers both his virgin daughter and the Levite's concubine to distract the village ruffians from an act of homosexual male rape of his dinner guest. Unlike the episode at Sodom and Gomorrah, the Gibeah roughnecks are satisfied by heterosexually ravaging (raping) and murdering the concubine but decline the old man's virgin daughter.

After taking his concubine home, the Levite dissects the now deceased woman into twelve pieces, one for each of the twelve tribes of the territory of Israel. He sends out the dismembered body with a note denouncing the abusive sexual terrorism, "Has such a thing ever happened since the day that the Israelites came up out from the land of Egypt until this day? Consider it, take counsel, and speak out" (19:30).

Von Rad, Gray, Boling, and Williams speak of the parallelism and the "distant dependence" (Von Rad) of the Gibeah and Sodom stories. "In both cases the sign of inhospitality is homosexual rape. That the men of Gibeah are not homosexuals is clear from their abuse of the concubine. Their intention, however, is vile in part because of the proposed subjection of the Levite to sexual rape. Here both he and his sexual identity would be violated. This sin also clearly contradicts Genesis 1–2 and the Levitical Laws."[10]

**2.** *Revisionist Interpretation.* Bailey's position asserts that sexuality is not the issue, certainly not homosexual rape. He declares that the pericope is one of an "anti-Saul polemic."[11] The revisionists have little further to say about the Gibeah rape, since the incidents at Gibeah and Sodom are roughly parallel. Therefore the reasoning is correspondingly similar.

**3.** *Discussion.* We find more sexual language in Judges 19 than in the story of Sodom. Clearly "to know" refers to a desire for sexual intercourse. Likewise, to "ravish" technically means to rape. The connotation of inhospitality is clearly more dreadful than any social insensitivity at mealtime. The intention of the Benjaminites is first homosexual rape, then heterosexual rape of a woman and her murder. The Levite fears that the ultimate goal of the Benjaminites is to murder him at Gibeah (20:5).

## The Holiness Codes: Leviticus 18:22-23; 20:13

**1.** *Traditional Interpretation.* The Levitical laws in the Holiness Code are priestly laws that call Israel to its highest and best, and are expressed in the formula, "This is the thing which the Lord has commanded" (Leviticus 17:1-2). God's transcendent holiness is communicated through the law. Israel's behavior individually and corporately quite literally is an expression of its fidelity to the transcendent holiness of God. Eichrodt observes that Israel, in the Levitical law and the Holiness Code, is commanded to conduct itself in such a way as to distinguish

its life from the surrounding pagan world. In short, the
Israelites are to be God's holy or sanctified people.[12]

In both 18:22 and 20:13 homosexuality is judged an abomination to the Lord. The traditionalists Noth[13] and Eichrodt claim
that the inveighing against homosexuality in 18:22 and 20:13 is
more than a prohibition of homosexuality and idolatrous acts. At
a deeper level, the prohibition includes anything that would
appear idolatrous and take away from the holiness of Israel's
relationship with God. Specifically, the prohibition against
homosexuality as an abomination occurs because homosexual
acts violate the holiness of the creation act itself. Williams, for
example, claims "homosexual acts are an abomination not
because of pagan cults, but because they reverse the natural order
of sexuality. In so doing they manifest the spirit of idolatry,
'which is itself [the] fundamental subversion of true order.'"[14]

The traditionalists claim that homosexual acts violate the
order of creation and violate divine will. As a consequence
homosexual acts are an abomination. Laws that prohibit homosexual acts are not cultic or cultural but theological and
revealed. Therefore they must be obeyed to honor the holiness
of God.[15] We also have the commentary, "Similarly in Leviticus
18:23 a woman lying with a beast is a 'perversion,' or literally a
'confusion.'"[16]

**2.** *Revisionist Interpretation.* McNeill, Bailey, Snaith, and
Scanzoni and Mollenkott interpret Levitical law and the Holiness Code to refer to the abomination of idolatry. To behave in
a homosexual way is to violate a cultic sexual code. Snaith
claims that the word *abomination* is used to refer to idolatrous
activities with other gods. Therefore homosexual behavior "is
condemned on account of its being associated with idolatry."[17]

Scanzoni and Mollenkott argue that if we are to take this text
legalistically, homosexuality cannot be separated from the
Israelite Holiness Code against the common twentieth-century
practices such as "eating rare steak, wearing mixed fabrics, and
having marital intercourse during the menstrual period."[18]

**3.** *Discussion.* The traditionalists claim that the Leviticus passages refer supremely to homosexual acts as an abomination to the created order as declared in Genesis 1–3. The revisionists link the prohibition of homosexual acts to idolatry in general. Their claim is that one must understand the cultural and social context of Israel's efforts to live a pure life in the midst of a pagan and adulterous, idolatrous world in which heterosexual and homosexual prostitution were part and parcel of the cultic rituals. Therefore we need to understand the prohibitions within the limited historical and theological context in which these passages are written. The issue is whether one chooses the more traditional and conservative interpretation of the Holiness of God and its demands upon Israel or the revisionists' efforts to locate the emphasis on the abomination of idolatry.

## CONCLUSION

As strongly as we may feel about the Old Testament and homosexuality, we must consider more than one point of view and appreciate more deeply the commitment to one's own view—or perhaps be changed and persuaded by an alternative view. Study and consultation with additional commentaries is needed to achieve a fuller grasp of the magnitude of the theological, sexual, and moral issues involved in this topic.

# CHAPTER 5

# The New Testament and Homosexuality

## Introduction

W e assume that Old and New Testaments are linked in a continuity of historical and theological traditions. They form the corpus for what Christianity refers to as the Judeo-Christian tradition. The New Testament writings, especially the words of Jesus in the Gospels and Paul's pastoral letters, build upon the writings, influence, and experience of the Old Testament and their efforts to translate and apply these teachings. The theological, socioeconomic, intellectual, moral, and sexual contexts of the New Testament are highly complex.

The Old Testament passages that deal directly with homosexuality come from early writings, including the Holiness Code, which is thought to be preexilic. During its early period, Israel was a compact theological and cultural entity. The exile occurred approximately 586 B.C. Between then and approximately A.D. 100, a period that includes the writing of most New Testament passages, an extraordinary amount of change occurred, spanning the rise and fruition of the Greco-Roman Empire, the coming of Christ, the whole New Testament period. Therefore, the setting or context within which one understands the moral and spiritual teachings of the Judeo-Christian tradition is much more complicated in A.D. 100 than in 586 B.C.

There are, however, some basic moral and sexual assumptions held in common by Old and New Testament writers.

First, both testaments assume that heterosexuality is normative for creation and assume that heterosexuality is essential for the sanctity of marriage. The prohibition against adultery as well assumes that heterosexuality is normative.

Second, Old Testament teachings on marriage, adultery, and homosexuality essentially are accepted by New Testament believers as foundational to the new Kingdom. Therefore discussion about homosexuality occupies little space in the New Testament writings. If homosexuality were a matter of controversy, conflict, or a point of contention, and had Jesus introduced a fundamentally new sexual ethic regarding heterosexual and homosexual behavior, debate clearly would occupy a more central position both in the Gospel accounts and the pastoral concerns of the New Testament.

The most extended discussion about sexual behavior including matters involving homosexuality comes from the writings of Paul directed to the Greco-Roman world, specifically at Corinth where Paul founded the church, and at Rome. Paul had not been to Rome when he wrote Romans. Nonetheless he was familiar with Rome's value system. Paul's discussion about sexual conduct and misconduct is subservient to his pastoral concern that nothing stand in the way of either Jew or Gentile receiving the grace of God. Therefore, while matters of sexual conduct are important teachings in their own right, one must always see the larger theological context in which moral and ethical behavior achieves its value. Receiving the forgiving grace of God and accepting new life in Christ enable one to live a morally exemplary life in the Christian community and in the larger social context.

In this chapter, three sections address New Testament teachings traditionally identified with homosexuality. As with the Old Testament sections in the preceding chapter, the *traditional* interpretation, the *revisionist* interpretation, and a *discussion* section will be presented in each case. We begin with the *traditional* to set the background for the contemporary discussion and to inform the reader of the dominant historical interpretations of these key Bible passages. In the section on the *revisionist* interpretation, the reader needs to understand the approach and the logic used by those who challenge the traditional interpretation of the passages in which the issue of homosexuality is central. The *discussion* section will endeavor to suggest to the reader how the issues may be joined for discussion and the kinds of theological, pastoral, and emotional concerns that remain unanswered or unsettled in the current debate between the traditional and the revisionist positions.

## The Gospels

The Gospel writers draw together the teachings of Jesus, the context of the early church, and focus on the most pressing and confusing of problems confronting the early church. They do not make explicit reference to or offer direct commentary about homosexuality. One must assume, from the absence of references to homosexuality in the Gospels and their focus on the pressing sexual issues in Jesus' ministry, divorce and adultery, that homosexuality per se does not constitute a central moral or theological controversy in the Gospels.[1]

In dealing with topics of adultery (Matthew 5:27-28) and divorce (Matthew 19:4-6; also Mark 10:2-9), Jesus draws upon an unchallenged presupposition for his life and that of his followers—including his Pharisee antagonist—that heterosexual marriage is normative:

> He answered, "Have you not read that the one who made them from the beginning 'made them male and female' and said, 'For this reason a man shall leave his father and mother and be joined to his wife and the two shall become one flesh'?" (Matthew 19:4-5)

Further, the only alternative Jesus offers to heterosexual marriage is celibacy or making oneself a "eunuch" for the Kingdom (Matthew 19:12; see also Paul in 1 Corinthians 7:27).

When Jesus refers to Sodom and Gomorrah, he does not focus on the sexual character of Sodom's sin. Rather he uses the two cities as an example of what happens to those who reject God's mighty works of redemption on the day of judgment (Matthew 10:15; 11:23-24). Sodom and Gomorrah become graphic, negative reminders of what is in store for those who reject the gospel. God doles out judgment through fire and brimstone "on the day when the Son of man is revealed" (Luke 17:29-30).

Williams observes that in the period when the Gospels were written, Sodom and Gomorrah symbolized coldness of heart and spiritual arrogance regarding the power and the judgment of God. However, by the time of the Dispersion (A.D. 64), when the Jews were confronted by Hellenistic homosexuality, Jewish literature employs Sodom and Gomorrah as notorious for their sexual misconduct.[2]

In brief, in the Gospels, conventional Jewish piety and marital law are simply assumed to apply: "Therefore a man leaves his father and his mother and clings to his wife, and they become one flesh" (Genesis 2:24). The heterosexual marriage is the paradigm. Likewise, Jewish laws regarding adultery were considered to apply equally to the Christian in the formation of marital ethics in the New Testament.

Homosexuality explicitly is not mentioned, but not because Jesus introduced a new ethic. Rather the radical continuity between Old and New Testament on this matter is a theological assumptive value held by Jesus and shared by the Gospel writers, other New Testament writers, and their audiences.

### Romans 1:26-27

**1.** *Traditional Interpretation.* The book of Romans has been considered the most systematic presentation of Paul's understanding of the gospel. In part, Romans deals most directly with doctrinal issues. These issues are presented in general and systematic terms, not pastoral terms, because at the time he wrote

Romans, Paul had not visited Rome. Unlike the pastoral letters (Corinthians, Galatians, Colossians) that address particular pastoral problems in churches Paul had visited or helped to found, the ethical and theological issues in Romans are not uniquely Roman pastoral problems but are properly seen as more general themes for the early church and the presentation of the gospel.[3]

Romans 1:26-27 must be seen in the context of the general preamble (1:16-17) that begins the larger section, 1:18–3:20. Salvation is given as the free gift of God's righteousness (1:16-17). Paul stresses the need of all people for the saving grace of God. In fact, in his summary, Paul declares there is no distinction between the Jews and the Gentiles when it comes to matters of salvation, unrighteousness, and the need for God's grace, "since all have sinned and fall short of the glory of God" (3:22-23). All are justified by God's grace as a gift through Jesus Christ and not by anything that we do (3:24).

The purpose of this passage is to identify the taproot of sin—namely, human idolatry and wickedness, our rebellion against God. In this section and others, scholars comment on Paul's dependence on the Book of Wisdom, a kind of homiletical tract, given to an elevated rhetorical style. Somewhat as politicians today rely on speech writers to provide one-liners, quotable quotes, and hard-hitting images, Paul depended on this theological speech writer. This fact does not diminish the weight of his argument, but today's readers of Romans 1–3 should be aware of Paul's rhetorical devices and not become so captivated by them that we fail to understand the higher theological message: We all sin and fall short of the glory of God. Only God's holiness, through Christ's grace, can save us from our sins. The cataloging of specific sins is a secondary or supportive device to underscore the major theological point. Whether Jew or Gentile, male or female, educated or unschooled, we cannot save ourselves.

As explained earlier (chapter 4), the word *homosexual* does not appear in the ancient texts of the Bible. (The word is found in more recent translations.) Scholars with a traditional interpretation of Romans 1:26-27 recognize that the word *unnatural* may refer to unusual, bizarre, even exotic social customs. But its specific theological reference is to homosexual activities. Further, in this passage is the first and only explicit recognition of and judgment upon female homosexuality ("Their women exchanged natural relations for unnatural").

While the language of Romans 1:26-27 may appear ambiguous to a modern reader, the theological and moral intent of the passage is not. It includes both male and female homosexuality. Further, in this overall discussion (1:18–3:23) the focus remains on sinful *behavior* ("Men committing shameless acts with men"). The *descriptive* emphasis is on sinful behavior as it always is in theological discussion. Here the reason for the sinful behavior is also clearly implied: the loss of self-control, discipline, social accountability, spiritual integrity, and the like. This occurs because, in God's holy righteousness and righteous wrath, Paul asserts, God hands over human behavior to "dishonorable passions" (verse 26). In this case the dishonorable passions refer to unnatural or homosexual acts. The issue is not whether people have homosexual fantasies, thoughts, or feelings; they may or may not. The theological emphasis is on God's refusal any longer graciously to intercede through natural thought processes, self-control, or passionate restraint. Rather, God's divine no releases both Jews and Gentiles to the uncontrollability of their passions. In this context those passions exhibit themselves in homosexual *behavior*.

Later, Paul says, "God gave them up to a base mind and improper conduct" (verse 28). Paul then lists a theological grab bag of sins.

The unrighteousness of the Gentiles is only one sin among many listed (verses 29-32). In theological terms, the natural pattern of the created order and the divine intent and pattern for natural relations among men and women is to be heterosexual. The marriage covenant is to be honored (Genesis 2:24). Men and women are to join in one flesh that honors humanity and

God. This theological perspective, deeply ingrained in the Old Testament, forms the bedrock of Paul's argument. Regardless of his rhetorical flourishes in this passage, Paul's argument is systematically consistent.

2. *Revisionist Interpretation.* Bailey, McNeill, Scroggs,[4] and Scanzoni and Mollenkott interpret the word *natural* to suggest that Paul is not talking about ontological structures—that is, divine order of sexual being and reality itself. They hold to an interpretation that treats *natural* as descriptive of the traditional or customary practices within a given culture or society. When stress and strain of a shift from traditional to nontraditional practices occur, frequently those who oppose the change term the shift unnatural. The logic of this sociological understanding is extended by Bailey to suggest that women exchanging natural for unnatural relations could involve unnatural heterosexual relations. One could assume that unnatural could refer to anything from adultery and its variants to any behavior including overt homosexual rape.

The revisionists make a radical distinction between the naturalness of social customs and theological naturalness as God's order of reality about sexual behaviors.

As an extension of this argument, McNeill draws upon contemporary psychological language to make a distinction between sexual *perversion* and sexual *inversion*. In brief, perversion would refer to a heterosexual who knowingly and self-consciously engages in sexual behaviors that violate known values, socialization influences, and so on. These could include both heterosexual perversions as well as homosexual perversions, but clearly they would be a self-conscious departure from a psychologically and sociologically perceived and experienced norm. *Inversion* is a clinical designation that refers to the claim of homosexuals that they have never had a heterosexual fantasy, thought, or feeling. The consistency of their emotional aversion to heterosexual activities and their consistently self-conscious feelings, thoughts, and intentions, claimed from birth to be directed exclusively toward same-sex people, is an inversion.[5]

By this clinical distinction, Bailey and others make a theological point that for the invert homosexual, sin would be to engage in the "unnatural" relations of heterosexual activity. For the homosexual invert, to engage in homosexual activity, whether one is male or female, is to honor natural relations, in Bailey's theology.

Therefore the revisionist would shift the general emphasis of this passage toward a psychological and sociological reading of Romans 1:18–3:23.

**3.** *Discussion.* In both the traditional and revisionist interpretations, one must be careful not to isolate Romans 1:26-27 from the larger theological context within which Paul writes. This theological/anthropological statement by Paul cannot be used in isolation from its theological context in which sins (however defined by traditionalists or revisionists) are not self-solving. For all have sinned and fall short of God's glory. Only God's grace extended through Jesus Christ can deliver us from a theological abandonment to uncontrolled passions, lusts, base mind, and improper conduct.

The difference is evident in how one chooses to link the social and historical context of Paul, the Judeo-Christian tradition in the Bible, and the Hellenistic customs of the time with the theological truth that is being offered and proclaimed in this passage. The revisionist will separate social custom from theological truth and weigh the balance of the argument accordingly. By contrast, the traditionalist will subordinate the social, economic, and political context to the theological truth being declared. The traditionalist will claim this passage describes the created order in which God's divine judgment against spiritual and moral rebellion is evident.[6]

## 1 Corinthians 6:9-11

**1.** *Traditional Interpretation.* The context of this pastoral letter is the Corinthian church in theological and moral disarray.

Chloe's followers plea for Paul to help them (1 Corinthians 1:11). First Corinthians 6 begins Paul's effort to remind the Corinthian "troops" of their high calling and to entreat them to stop arguing, fighting, and suing one another. The church is undisciplined and unspiritual. Paul appeals to a communal spiritual confidence and encourages the Corinthians to begin to sort things out. Running to the civil courts on religious matters only further inflames the conflict (6:1-7).

The apostle shows his holy anger over the intentional wrongs and mean spirit of the church. By 1 Corinthians 6:9, Paul admonishes that the unrighteous (spiritually stubborn, stiff-necked, unrepentant, mean-spirited) will not inherit the Kingdom of God.

This pastoral letter rings with practicality and specificity on sexual matters. We must conclude that Paul has specific acts and unrighteous attitudes in mind. In 1 Corinthians 6:9 he in effect declares, "Don't kid yourself. Your behavior and attitudes are sufficient to disqualify you from the Kingdom of God; and I'm not kidding. You ought to know better. When you were saved, you came from pagan backgrounds. By the grace of the Lord Jesus Christ, you were cleansed and justified. Don't backslide!"

Scholars have remarked that the catalog of sins (6:9b-10) is from a standard theological and homiletical list comparable to the one used in Romans 1, Galatians 5, and 1 Timothy 1.[7] While the parallel to other passages exists, we cannot dismiss the significance of the specific references to homosexuality as sexual immorality.

Beginning with the RSV, the word *homosexual* has been used in this catalog. The English is based upon a compound of two Greek words, the passive (*malakos*—"pervert," "effeminate") and the active (*arsenokoites*—"sodomite"). The traditional interpretation of the linking of these two words is a prohibition against both the *passive* homosexual partner (*malakos*) and the *active* homosexual partner (*arsenokoites*). The traditionalists are not willing to soften their interpretation of the RSV coinage of *homosexual* to suggest simply general, nonspecific immoral behavior. The argument is straightforward. The word *immoral* is used as a generic term at the beginning of the passage. The terms *malakos* and *arsenokoites* are included in the list of specific sins: idolatry, adultery, thievery, greed, drunkenness, and robbery. In this context, homosexual must be taken in its sexual sense of referring specifically to those engaged in homosexual oral or anal sexual acts. The sin then is doubly exposed.[8] It is wrong to give oneself *both* to passive homosexual acts *and* to active homosexual acts.

Following this harsh listing of sins for the Corinthian Christians, the apostle offers a reassuring word of hope (verse 11): Justification and sanctification are available through Christ, regardless of sins committed—if one repents. Sin, chaos, and immoral behaviors do not have to have the last word. The Gospel does, if we but hear.[9]

**2.** *Revisionist Tradition.* McNeill, Bailey, Scroggs, Scanzoni and Mollenkott, and Boswell[10] take exception to the traditionalists at two major points. First, they say the catalog of sins is a generic listing used elsewhere in the New Testament. Second, the Greek words *malakos* and *arsenokoites* do not refer to homosexual activities but rather to more general inappropriate moral behavior. Boswell claims *malakos* refers to effeminate, "soft," weak personalities, and *not* to passive homosexual partners. In fact, in discussing this point, McNeill argues that "the majority of male homosexuals prefer manliness in themselves and their partners. Further, most transvestites and males with effeminate characteristics are as a matter of fact heterosexually inclined."[11] Extending this logic, Scroggs declares the force of this passage is aimed at pederasty, a practice of sexual activity between adult males and boys. Pederasty was practiced in the Greco-Roman world. Even if one defines *malakos* as self-indulgent, narcissistic self-centeredness, the proper understanding of *arsenokoites* is restricted in its meaning of application to male homosexual prostitutes. It is for Boswell, McNeill, and other revisionists limited in its theological scope to male homosexual prostitutes and not applied to the general population. This position would claim that as long as a Christian is not self-indulgent or a homosexual prostitute, the language and the intention of the biblical passage do not apply to congenial, loving *philia* and *eros* expressions of affection between consenting same-sex adult males.

The revisionist argument insists that *malakos* and *arsenokoites* are generic references to sexual misconduct. Male prostitution and pederasty at Corinth are included in the "harsh list" to be sure but not homosexual behavior in general. A second disagreement for the revisionists is their claim that *arsenokoites* refers exclusively to male prostitutes and therefore excludes homosexual behavior in general from the sins list in 1 Corinthians 9:9. The third exception claimed by the revisionists is that the language of the passage is not sexually oriented. Therefore the catalog of wickedness and evil does not include sexuality.

An additional exegetical comment is offered by Victor Furnish. He notes that nowhere is a plural ending attached to the word *sin*. Numerous catalogs of wickedness, evil, and unrighteousness exist. Paul uses the word *sin* in contrast with other early church traditions: there is only one sin (singular) and that is the power that drives a wedge between God and God's people. This observation is more dramatically demonstrated in 1 Corinthians than in the Romans 1 passage because 1 Corinthians 6 deals with those sins that separate the believer from God. The Romans 1 passage is focused primarily on sexual behavior.[12]

**3.** *Discussion.* Three points of contention exist between the traditionalists and the revisionists. First is the conflict over whether the language of the passage refers directly and specifically to sexual activities or is more properly understood as wickedness and evil of a general nature. A second conflict occurs in understanding the 1 Corinthians 6 catalog as being similar to the list in Romans 1, Galatians 5, and 1 Corinthians 5. Is Paul being specific about homosexual behavior or is he simply being preachy in his use of words to illustrate sin? The third and most critical point of dispute arises over the combination of two Greek words, *malakos* and *arsenokoites*. Do they refer to male prostitutes or to adult homosexual partners?

Paul's catalog and language come from a common literary source. His imagery in 1 Corinthians 6 and in Romans 1 is influenced by a rhetorical style seen in the Book of Wisdom. The selection of the two Greek words translated as "homosexual" in the RSV and "male prostitutes" in the NRSV seems appropriate for meaning of Paul's singular intensity. He would not likely choose his words thoughtlessly or carelessly in discussing such a controversial issue with the Corinthian Christians. The rabbinic formula Paul uses provides for—as we see in the other passages where the catalog is used—addition, subtraction, and omission without theological violation. Given the general sexual and cultural context of Corinth, the seriousness of the sins, and the factious infighting addressed in 1 Corinthians 6, the evidence of both context and literary sources suggests that Paul chose his words carefully. The next issue is the proper translation of the combination of Greek words. The commonsense conclusion dictates that the wickedness addressed is adult male homosexual anal intercourse.

This behavior plus the other behaviors cataloged in the passage are totally unacceptable for Paul personally and for the general spiritual well-being of the Corinthian church. The pastoral concern and the theological admonition is for Corinthian Christians to regain their first love and theologically regroup under the Lordship of Jesus Christ. Let go of these various sins and get on with the upbuilding of the Kingdom of God in the congregation.

## 1 Timothy 1:8-11; Jude, Verse 7

**1.** *Traditional Interpretation.* In 1 Timothy the catalog of vices used in Romans 1 and 1 Corinthians 6 is invoked again in Paul's letter to the young pastor Timothy. In listing behaviors that vio-

late the law first, Paul draws upon a rhetorical structure similar
to the Ten Commandments.[13] The passage, unlike Romans and
1 Corinthians, is addressed specifically to nonbelievers. In 1 Timothy 1:8, Paul declares, "Now we know that the law is good, if
one uses it legitimately." First Timothy 1 reiterates the same
theological theme: the law is revealed in the Ten Commandments and in the "natural design" of the universe as expressed
in Genesis 1 and 2. First Timothy 1:10 uses "sodomites" as a
vice similar to the sin cataloged in 1 Corinthians 6:9.

Based upon the Levitical law and Holiness Code, *sodomite*
refers to a male having sex with other males.[14] The traditionalists claim that the theological and behavioral reference in
1 Timothy 1:9 is to male homosexual behavior. The only difference between the more significant statements in Romans 1 and
1 Timothy is that the 1 Timothy 1:9 catalog is also addressed to
those who are not a part of the household of faith and are dis-
obedient to the law against homosexuality.

Likewise in Jude 7, the reference to Sodom and Gomorrah
coupled with "unnatural lust" (*sarkos heteras*), or "wrong kind
of flesh," theologically refers to a violation of the natural order
of heterosexuality. The significance of Jude 7 for the traditionalist is the clear linkage and witness to the *sexual nature* of the
Sodom and Gomorrah wickedness.

**2.** *Revisionist Interpretation.* The revisionist position would
argue that in Romans 1:26-27, 1 Corinthians 6:9, 1 Timothy 1:10,
and Jude 7, "same-sex abuses refer to specific kinds of acts rather
than to the condition of being homosexual." Especially in 1 Timothy 1:8-11, the condemnation of those who live outside the law,
the evil or wickedness described is not homosexual orientation
but same-sex abuses. Therefore, according to Scanzoni and Mollenkott, "to tell homosexuals on the basis of this passage [1
Corinthians 6:11] that to enter God's kingdom they must cease to
be homosexual, or at least cease expressing their homosexuality,
is to place them under the law rather than under grace." The
authors continue, "Homosexuals cannot earn salvation by the
sacrifice of their sexuality any more than heterosexuals can."[15]

**3.** *Discussion.* The conflict between the revisionists and the traditionalists surfaces over several points. Do these passages overall refer to sins of inhospitality as argued for the Sodom/Gomorrah pericope? Or do they refer explicitly to male homosexual behavior? A second conflict arises over the intent of the language: Does it refer specifically to homosexual behavior or to homosexual attitudes or affective orientation? The revisionists believe that Paul's words of condemnation refer to sexual perversions that are distortions of one's natural, loving sexual orientation. They claim these passages do not refer explicitly to the sexual invert or the "true" homosexual. The sin in both the Old and New Testaments is one of violence and violation of one's being.

The revisionists argue that the Bible is silent about loving, affectionate relationships of same-sex partners who genuinely (both in attitude and in behavior) are in love with each other. The perversion and violence associated with these various acts of ungodliness, wickedness, and evil are principally and fundamentally a defiance and defilement of the Holiness of God and the intended order of creation, including heterosexual love and nonviolent behavior toward others, whether homosexual or heterosexual. Only at a secondary theological level do the violence and wickedness explicitly involve sexual sins. Our sin against God is the greater sin, regardless of the behavior. All human beings created in the image of God have the breath of life and are called by God to conform to the paradigm or the created order as witnessed to in Genesis 1 and 2.

## CONCLUSION

As stated at the beginning of this and the preceding chapter, homosexuality is not a major anthropological theme in either the Old or the New Testament. The Judeo-Christian tradition, theologically, assumes heterosexuality to be the normative pattern; and certainly in the New Testament, Paul condemns homosexual practices but is not preoccupied with homosexual sins.

Four summary statements by Victor Furnish on the topic invite us to engage in a measured reflection on the topic. First, Furnish claims that Paul did not offer direct, explicit teaching in his pastoral letters on the subject of homosexual content. Therefore the passages considered do not afford immediate, specific answers to the questions of homosexuality in the contemporary situation.

Second, Paul shared in traditions of his Jewish background and "the wisdom of his day." His theological focus was drawn to the wickedness of homosexual practice principally in its lust and perversion of the natural order.

Third, Paul's essential theological concerns about homosexual practice remain, according to Furnish, as valid in the twentieth century as they were in the first. Essentially, homosexual practices represent rebellion against God the Creator and the creation.

Finally, and perhaps most significant, Paul's comments about the wickedness and vice of homosexual behavior dare not be isolated from the wider and more powerful theological context in which the behavior occurs. All our sins, whether homosexual practices or heterosexual practices or sins that have no overt sexual significance, place us in the category of sinners and at enmity with God. We are needful of God's grace revealed to us in and through Jesus Christ.[16]

# PART III

# A CONTEMPORARY
# PERSPECTIVE

# CHAPTER 6

# A Contemporary Debate on Homosexuality in the Church

T he principal focus of the debate on homosexuality is theological. What is our faith response to God supremely revealed in Jesus Christ, God's only Son (John 3:16)? How are we instructed, guided, inspired, and corrected by the teachings of Scriptures (2 Timothy 3:16-17)? Three major discussion points of the church's debate will be presented: (1) the theological issues, (2) the social science issues, and (3) ministerial leadership issues.

## Theological Issues

**1.** *Theology as Theology.* John Calvin was a Reformation theologian (1509–1564) whose writings and teachings are the cornerstone of Presbyterianism. In the opening paragraph of his *Institutes of the Christian Religion,* Calvin declares that theological study may begin with "the knowledge of God and of ourselves."[1] Calvin's theological reasoning asserts that the organizing center for all theological discussion and authority finally is God; it is not human experience.

Many aspects of Calvin's classical orthodoxy are shared by other Protestant reformers, Martin Luther (1483–1546) and John Wesley (1703–1791). These theologians used the ancient creeds of the Christian church, especially the Apostles' and Nicene Creeds as the theological point of departure for their preaching and writing. The holiness and otherness of God are lifted up in stark contrast to the sinful and depraved inability of human

beings to save themselves *except* by the grace of Jesus Christ.[2]
One consequence of classical orthodoxy is its emphasis upon
the weakness, sinfulness, and unworthiness of the human spirit.

By the early 1940s, American philosopher and theologian
Charles Hartshorne (b. 1897) advanced a theological corrective
to the good intentions but contradictory claims of the reformed
theologians. Hartshorne and his followers advocated a *neoclassical theism*.[3] His neoclassical or dipolar theism is his attempt
to establish a more properly balanced orthodoxy: God is the
supreme example of activity *and* passivity; God is the supreme
example of transcendence *and* immanence; God is the supreme
example of power *and* weakness (the incarnation). God is both
Absolute and Relative.

Both classical and neoclassical Christian orthodoxy insist
that "the reality of God" is *the* central focus of theology.[4]
Schubert Ogden declares,

> To be sure, I have already said enough in criticizing the theolo-
> gies of liberation to make clear why no theology can legitimate-
> ly focus solely on the existential meaning of God for us, to the
> exclusion of all considerations of the metaphysical being of God
> in himself. . . . It is just because, on the basis of the same apos-
> tolic witness, we both can and should understand our existence
> in the world in this distinctive way that we must understand the
> primal source and final end of our existence to be none other
> than the God and Father of Jesus Christ.[5]

**2.** *Theology as Praxis.* Many Christians are impatient with
the theological failure of classical orthodoxy and choose to
emphasize practice, or praxis, as the focus of Christian faith. A
major formulation of "theology as praxis" is liberation theology
with its focus on poverty. It declares that the Gospel's power is
to liberate persons from religious, social, and economic oppression. Liberation theologians such as Fred M. Herzog, James H.
Cone, and Jose Miguez Bonino[6] emphasize emancipation from
the powers that interfere with God's will for humanity.

Another example of "theology as practice" is the clinical

pastoral care movement. Begun in the 1930s, its emphasis upon an action/reflection theology is an effort to make eternal spiritual truths practical in efforts to meet human suffering.[7] The various theological efforts to make theology practical without turning it into sociology or psychology have made great advances for the church in its thought and ministry. But they also have created widespread controversy.

The emancipation and the action/reflection models are efforts to focus theology in practice, not just theoretical "God talk." Their chief criticism of classical orthodoxy is of its proclivity toward philosophical speculation about God.

**3.** *Theology as Sociology.* This is the most radical way to frame theological discussion. It goes beyond the action/reflection model and the emancipation/redemption model and locates redemption solely in psychological and sociological terms, not spiritual. This model pushes God away from being a transcendent other (orthodoxy) and God as mediator (action/reflection) to God as being strictly an economic, psychological, or political liberator. Radical theologians claim that the knowledge of God can only occur in empirical, sociological, and behavioral change. For them any nonpractical reflection about the metaphysical being of God, the inner witness of the Spirit, or a more prayerful and patient supplication before the holy triune God is blasphemy. Gutierrez and Alves tread on turning theology into sociology.[8]

In their theology of sexuality, the revisionists (McNeill, Boswell, Bailey) share a common view. John McNeill, in a chapter entitled "The Human Sciences and Homosexuality," expresses the need to abandon theological orthodoxy, which declares that heterosexuality is the created norm. Orthodoxy holds that homosexuality is a sin and a distortion of God's will, a view that theologically is unacceptable to the revisionists.

Having interpreted the Old Testament texts on homosexuality and sodomy as dealing strictly with problems of social inhospitality and having argued that New Testament references to sodomy and "unnatural relations" are limited to nonsexual acts, McNeill locates his theological argument in psychological and

sociological data. His protest really is over psychiatric orthodoxy, which claims homosexuality is aberrant, a perversion, and
a mental illness. McNeill states that his task is one of correcting
the psychiatrist and the sociologist as well as the theologian.

By shifting his focus to sociological and psychiatric discussions, McNeill in effect argues that theological orthodoxy, in
asserting that homosexuality is a sin, is irrelevant and superflu-
ous. McNeill is a psychotherapist and argues for a consistent,
radical shift from theological to psychiatric categories.[9]

In summary, the most important theological issue is, Where
does theology base its center: theological orthodoxy? Praxis
(action/reflection) model or paradigm? Are psychiatric and
sociological categories a correct theological center? If a theological position turns theology into sociology, it puts the theological cart before the horse. When theology becomes psychiatry and the social sciences become a substitute for the Apostles'
Creed along with other classic creeds and confessions of the
church, truly a radical shift has occurred.

## Social Science Issues

Next we consider how the contemporary debate on homosexuality in the church includes discussion from the social sciences.

**1.** *Sex as Polymorphous Perversity.* Sigmund Freud is considered the founder of modern psychology. He referred to the
human sex drive as "polymorphous perversity." He used this
terminology to convey his observation that humans do not have
an innate sex drive that is exclusively heterosexual. Freud used
this category in his therapeutic treatment to explain the significance of early childhood experience. We are sexually condi-
tioned through interaction with parents and their efforts to
adhere to ascribed social roles and to live according to specific
patterns of sexual behavior. We are not predetermined to be heterosexual, according to Freud, but rather we are open to a wide
variety of expressions of the human sex drive.

In his use of this terminology to explain human sex drive, Freud argued that among the lower animals, sex is controlled and directed by biological instinct toward heterosexual procreation and preservation of the species. Human behavior, including sex, is neither driven nor protected by the same instinctive boundaries. Therefore the objects of human sexual interest can be unlimited or polymorphous (poly=many; morphos=form). These objects may be one's own body, other human objects (opposite sex or same sex objects), or imaginary objects (fantasies of bodily, inanimate, or human love objects).

Freud uses the term *perversity* as a clinical designation. It signifies that humans have no innate sex drive that guarantees that one's sexual energies will always be directed toward a single type of sexual object. Masturbation, autoeroticism, sodomy (anal sex with subhuman species), homosexual relations, or any combination of a real or imagined sexual relationship with any real or imagined "love object" are all possible sources of human sexual gratification and pleasure. Freud's insight understood human sexual energy to be a quavering, unbounded packet of energy. Neither convention nor society nor innate biological devices or mechanisms will automatically direct humans in one specific direction or toward one specific type of object. As a Victorian, Freud's therapeutic goal was to help patients whose lives had become psychologically handicapped by their polymorphous perversity to redirect their sexual energy toward a more appropriate and healthy expression within the conventions of late nineteenth-century Victorian Viennese society.[10]

Freud's views on sexuality, while encapsulated in clinical imagery, run parallel to the freedom the theologian understands as being granted to Adam and Eve in Genesis 1–2. God gives no guarantees that human moral or sexual behavior will duplicate God's intention for us in creation: We have the freedom to choose good or evil. For the Christian, standards are established by the revelation of God in Jesus Christ, surrounded by the witness of Scripture and refined by the teaching of the church. For Freud there were no theological constructs. He saw society as

the ultimate determiner; thus, society is the context in which
moral and behavioral standards are formed.

**2.** *Repression and Sex Roles.* A lasting contribution of Freud's
psychological insights is his assertion that human behavior and values are determined by the traumas of early childhood experience.[11]

The norms for human sexual expression do not spring uncon-
tested from intellectual wonderment. For Freud, norms derive
from negative reinforcement, coercion, punishment, and catas-
trophic sexual threats to a child if obedience is not secured.
Fears of terrifying social and sexual consequences by a non-
compliant child produce what clinicians understand as repression of sexual energy. That trauma "motivates" children and
adults into rigid, repressed sexual behavior.

The homosexual community argues two points to advance its
position in the continuing conversation with Freudian thought and
insights. First, it follows Freud's argument that humans are essentially bisexual. Each of us has active sexual aspects, however
recessive, of the opposite sex. Therefore, the line of argument
goes, whether one becomes heterosexual or homosexual is primarily a matter of social conditioning. Humans as bisexual beings
endowed with polymorphous perversity can readily develop either
heterosexual or homosexual characteristics. The dominant cultural
values generally will direct an individual toward a heterosexual or
a homosexual orientation. The homophile community extends
Freud's observation that heterosexual behavior is repressed psy-
chic material, psychological residue of the unresolved Oedipal
complex. The repressed incestuous desires of the infant for the
parent are denied, and the denial is reinforced through the social
conventions by which people learn "correct" sexual behavior. In
the long tradition of Western culture, the repressed sexual instincts
are traumatically socialized to assure sexual behavior that is heterosexual. The appeal of this argument is its assumption that
humans are not created heterosexual or homosexual. Therefore if
one is truly liberated as a gay or lesbian, one's preference and
freedom to be homosexual is thereby released and should be
appropriately received in society.

The second fundamental claim of the gay community is that homosexuals are born gay and rejoice in their "God-given" homosexuality.

But are these not contradictory views? One position suggests that sex roles are determined by emotional trauma, and the other view holds that one is born homosexual. Is homosexuality a learned behavior or not? That's the issue.[12] The debate over this conflict consumed the psychological and therapeutic communities of the American Psychiatric Association during the late 1960s and early 1970s; and the debate was furious. Is one's sexual orientation learned or innate? The debate is too powerful to be resolved in a few brief years. In 1973 the landmark action of the American Psychiatric Association occurred. While the debate within the ranks of the APA continues and the discussion outside of psychiatric circles is undiminished, no new action or decision has been made since that date. Therefore, when the American Psychiatric Association membership voted to remove homosexuality from its official list of mental diseases in 1973, history was made.

**3.** *American Psychiatric Association Debate.* In an extensive study, *Homosexuality and American Psychiatry: The Politics of Diagnosis,* released in 1981, Ronald Bayer attempted to put the dispute of the American Psychiatric Association in a historical perspective. The first paragraph in Bayer's introduction summarizes the setting for this debate:

In 1973, after several years of bitter dispute, the Board of Trustees of the American Psychiatric Association decided to remove homosexuality from the *Diagnostic and Statistical Manual of Psychiatric Disorders,* its official list of mental diseases. Infuriated by that action, dissident psychiatrists charged the leadership of their association with an unseemly capitulation to the threats and pressures of Gay Liberation groups, and forced the board to submit its decision to a referendum of the full APA membership. And so America's psychiatrists were called to vote upon the question of whether homosexuality ought to be considered a mental disease. The entire process, from the first confrontations organized by gay demonstrators at psychiatric conventions to the referendum demanded by orthodox psychiatrists, seemed to violate the most basic expectations about how questions of science should be resolved. Instead of being engaged in a sober consideration of data, psychiatrists were swept up in a political controversy. The American Psychiatric Association had fallen victim to the disorder of a tumultuous era, when disruptive conflicts threatened to politicize every aspect of American social life.[13]

Several significant factors surface in Bayer's summary of a decade-long debate. First, the decision by the APA to "downgrade" the diagnostic category of homosexuality was *not based upon new scientific evidence or a breakthrough in therapeutic treatment*. Rather, as Bayer states, "while the homosexual revolt against heterosexual domination mirrored the process of social upheaval on the part of the marginal, disenfranchised groups, the assault upon psychiatry must be viewed as echoing the contemporary attack on what had been, until the 1960s, the unassailable status of science and technology, medicine in particular."[14] The gay liberation groups were an active force in the 1973 changes.

A second and perhaps complementing factor was a changing of the guard in the orthodox psychiatric power structure, giving way to a "reformist" posture. A third factor was the medical confusion that resulted from the APA becoming so embroiled in an essentially political—not a scientific—controversy. A fourth element was the pressure by the gay lobby to shift the discussion from moral language to a clinical and diagnostic language base.

Psychiatric orthodoxy had long been persuaded that homosexuality was a developmental issue and therefore considered homosexuality—for better or for worse—a mental illness. The gay liberation movement, linked to the political momentum of the civil rights movement of the 1960s, nurtured a "gay is good" momentum. Its initial appeal was to the homophile movement, encouraging its followers to engage in ideological confrontations such as voting. By 1970 The Gay Liberation

Front was not as effective as it might have been, because of excessive ideological orthodoxy.[15]

Champions of the revision (Judd Marmor, Martin Hoffman, and Richard Green, among others) argued that "the classification of homosexuality as a mental illness represented nothing more than the cloaking of moral judgments in the language of science." Many psychiatrists and other mental health professionals were "beginning to doubt the merits of classifying homosexuality as a disease." Following the New York gay activist alliance rally on October 8, 1972, a "full-scale effort to demand the amendment of the *Diagnostic and Statistical Manual of Psychiatric Disorders (DSM-II)*" was mounted.[16] At the May 1973 APA convention, Robert Spitzer emerged as a central figure in the debate. He was convinced that "the inclusion of homosexuality in the *DSM-II* constituted an unjustified extension of the concept of 'psychiatric disorder.'" Spitzer recommended a new classification, "sexual orientation disturbance."[17]

The controversy raged over six months (May–December 1973), with the APA approving the deletion of homosexuality as a disease and replacing the *DSM-II* classification with the classification "sexual orientation disturbance." Critics of the vote to support Spitzer's wording argued vehemently that psychiatry is a scientific discipline. As a subspecialty of medicine, it had engaged in "diagnostic politics" in its decision to delete homosexuality as a psychiatric disorder. To the critics opposed to the change, the reason for reclassification was transparent: "Having forsaken the canons of science, psychiatry had revealed itself to be a subdivision of theology, its board having behaved 'like a church council deciding on matters of dogma.'"[18] To further politicize the process, opponents of the change, such as John Socarides and Irving Bieber, prevailed on the APA to circulate a referendum on homosexuality asking people to indicate support or opposition to the board's decision. Out of more than 10,000 ballots cast, 58 percent supported the board, 37 percent were opposed.[19]

In a vitriolic denunciation of the revision, Jonas Robitscher declared that "the generation of younger psychiatrists brought up on the new official position will inevitably see Marmor's position as the 'scientific' point of view and the older position if they learn about it at all as 'outmoded,' 'old-fashioned' and 'unscientific.'"[20]

Further controversy resolved itself formally in 1977 with the adoption of a new category, "ego-dystonic homosexuality":

> A desire to acquire or increase heterosexual arousal so that het-
> erosexual relations can be initiated or maintained and a sustained
> pattern of overt homosexual arousal that the individual explicitly
> complains is unwanted as a source of distress.[21]

Further, the new manual *(DSM-III)* would read:

> Since homosexuality itself is not considered a mental disorder,
> the factors that predispose to homosexuality are not included in
> this section. The factors that predispose to ego-dystonic homo-
> sexuality are those negative societal attitudes towards homosexu-
> ality which have been internalized. In addition features associat-
> ed with heterosexuality such as having children and socially
> sanctioned family life, may be viewed as desirable, and incom-
> patible with a homosexual arousal pattern.[22]

Significant for our purposes is the implication of the subtitle of the Bayer book, "The Politics of Diagnosis." Robitscher warned that the change in the *DSM-III* was not based upon new scientific evidence, and that the charges brought against the older *DSM-II* that it was unscientific clearly is not the case. Change to the *DSM* occurred, but not by an increase in scientific understanding. Rather it was a protracted and controversial political process within the APA that forced the change. One may agree or disagree with the APA decision in December 1973. The question of whether the change was essentially a scientific or an ideological decision seems obvious. Therefore, we are led to conclude that the debate before and after the 1973

APA decision to delete homosexuality from its classification as a mental disorder was a political process not a scientific one.

In brief, much of modern psychology is based upon the theoretical and clinical work of Sigmund Freud. Clinicians have struggled for a hundred years trying to understand better the complexity and intensity of human sexual behavior. That we are not predisposed toward a single sexual, instinctual direction seems clearly established. That there are very subtle developmental issues that surround one's bisexuality is also clear. Sex role socialization behavior of parents and care-taking figures, as well as the interplay of other powerful developmental forces suggest that the early APA *DSM-II* classification of homosexuality as a mental disorder may have been an overstatement. But the political pressure, including a successful call for a referendum by those dissatisfied with the 1973 vote, makes it abundantly clear that the decision by the APA in 1973 to change its classification was not a scientific one. In part a political one, in part an ideological decision, in part a moral choice, in part a social sensitivity response, the action clearly was not a scientific conclusion.

## Ministerial Leadership Issues

Despite the recent contoversy over homosexuality registered by both the homophobic and homophilic movements, among the mainline Protestant denominations there has never been a widespread orthodoxy that prevents homosexuals from attending and participating in the ongoing life of a local congregation. The issue of controversy has focused on two important theological elements: (1) ministerial ordination and (2) behavioral emulation of church leaders. A fuller discussion of these two areas of the controversy is in order.

**1.** *Ministerial Ordination.* Church historian Richard F. Lovelace, in *Homosexuality in the Church: Crises, Conflict and Compassion,* presents a succinct social, theological, and political summary of the issue of the ordination of homosexuals.[23] In the 1948 release *Sexual Behavior in the Human Male,* Alfred

Kinsey suggested that homosexuality was more widespread than commonly thought and that many practices common among the homosexual community were employed in heterosexual behavior. This study had its impact on both the theological and the medical community. By 1954, Anglican clergy D. S. Bailey published *Homosexuality and the Western Christian Tradition,* in which he proposed "that homosexual behavior between consenting adults in private be no longer a criminal offence."[24] By the early sixties several homophile organizations, including the Gay Liberation Movement and the Council on Religion and the Homosexual, were conceived at Glide Memorial [United] Methodist Church in San Francisco.

By 1968 Troy Perry, a minister with Assemblies of God credentials and background, became the founder of the Metropolitan Community Church of Los Angeles. A year later Dignity, an organization for gay Catholics, was formed by Father Pat Nidorf. In 1972 William Johnson was ordained by the United Church of Christ; and in 1973 the National Task Force on Gay People was recognized by the governing board of the National Council of the Churches of Christ in the U.S.A. A year earlier the Episcopal Church denied ordination to "an affirmed gay seminarian" and the United Methodist General Conference in its Statement of Social Principles (1972) declared, "We do not condone the practice of homosexuality and consider this practice incompatible with Christian doctrine." This landmark statement first incorporated in paragraph 72.C of the 1972 *Discipline* has remained essentially intact through the 1988 *Discipline* (paragraph 71.F). One change that does indicate change in substance occurs: In 1972 "homosexual" is used as a noun which may suggest that one is a homosexual by birth. In the 1988 *Discipline* "homosexual" is used as an adjective in "homosexual persons." This suggests that homosexuality may be a modifying condition, not a permanent one.

In 1970 a position paper was presented to the General Assembly of The United Presbyterian Church in the U.S.A. (UPCUSA) that argued for the Assembly's approval of both homosexual and extramarital sexual relations, but it was rejected. In 1975 the General Assembly formalized its data by establishing a gay Presbyterian task force, but it was unacceptable to the commissioners. In 1976 the New York Presbytery submitted a formal petition to the General Assembly to receive "guidance" on whether or not to ordain a self-avowed sexually active homosexual candidate. Among Episcopalians, in 1975 the ordination of Ellen Marie Barrett, a self-declared homosexual, by Bishop Paul Moore of New York resulted in a 1976 General Convention establishment of a three-year study on homosexuality. This Standing Commission on Human Affairs and Health had a mandate to "study in depth the matter of ordination of homosexual persons and report its findings and recommendations . . . to the next General Convention." Following the commission's report at the Sixty-sixth General Convention (1977), the Convention adopted a resolution that stated several conditions required "in the selection and approval of persons for ordination." Among these the following two pertain to this discussion: "(1) Every ordinand is expected to lead a life which is 'a wholesome example to all people' (*Book of Common Prayer,* pp. 517, 532, 544). There should be no barrier to the ordination of either heterosexual or homosexual orientation whose behavior the church considers wholesome; (2) we reaffirm the traditional teaching of the Church on marriage, marital fidelity and sexual chastity as the standards of Christian sexual morality. Candidates for ordination are expected to conform to this standard. Therefore, we believe it is not appropriate for this Church to ordain a practicing homosexual, or any person who is engaged in heterosexual relations outside of marriage."[25]

In his essay "Decorum as Doctrine: ECUSA's Recent Teachings on Human Sexuality," Harmon Smith, professor of moral theology at Duke University, has helped, through his research, to put this debate in proper perspective:

The limiting clause, which asserts that "it is not appropriate for this Church to ordain a practicing homosexual, or any person

who is engaged in heterosexual relations outside of marriage,''
identifies two disqualifying standards; it also provokes much of
the friction, if not enmity, which now marks discussion of human
sexuality in this Church. The internal logic of the resolution,
however, is consistent: human sexual intercourse is restricted to
marriage, and marriage is restricted to couples which are com-
posed of one man and one woman.[26]

In 1976 Father John McNeill called for reconsideration of the
traditional attitudes on homosexuality within the Roman
Catholic Church. A year later, McNeill was ordered not to teach
or preach on the subject publicly. His book *The Church and the
Homosexual* was ordered withdrawn.

By the mid-1970s the debate was especially intense among
the mainline denominations. In all likelihood the watershed
decision was made at the 1978 assembly of the UPCUSA, when
the General Assembly voted overwhelmingly in support of a
twelve-page committee report that included "definitive guidance" for the New York Presbytery based upon its 1976 request
for guidance, regarding the ordination request of William Sil-
ver, the self-affirmed homosexual ministerial candidate under
Care of Presbytery. The intense debate that ensued from 1976
to 1978 is signaled by the fact that the committee's minority
report (five of nineteen members) was persuasive among the
delegates and reflected the sentiments of many "overtures"
submitted by local presbyteries. A redrafting of the majority
report was accomplished at the San Diego General Assembly
(May 1978), at which an acceptable document was perfected
and adopted. Under the political tutelage of Josiah Beeman, a
compromise report was adopted that would provide guidance to
the New York Presbytery and the church.

After all debate had been completed, principal leaders from
both sides of the issue were summoned to the podium to join in
prayer for the sake of the church and its ministry.[27] In its discussion, deliberation, and theological conclusions, three factors
emerged that have served as landmarks both for the Presbyteri-

an Church U.S.A. and other Protestant churches that have been engaged in the same type of discussion and debate during the 1970s, 1980s, and 1990s.

First, a theological position surfaced that explicitly forbade the ordination of self-affirmed, practicing homosexuals. Second, a deliberate effort not to engage in sexual witch hunts was in evidence. Third, a renewed call to work on behalf of the civil rights of homosexuals that would "prohibit discrimination in the areas of employment, housing, public accommodation based upon the sexual orientation of a person" was heard.

Because most of the mainline denominations had been active in the drive for the civil rights of black Americans during the 1960s and 1970s, the national leadership as expressed both by the elected leaders of the boards and agencies as well as the representative leadership (delegates and commissioners, etc.) elected to go on record in support of the *civil* rights of gays and lesbians but not the *ordination* claims of gays and lesbians. In part this was in reaction to the much celebrated Dade County, Florida, controversy over the civil rights of homosexual teachers and Anita Bryant's highly visible quasi-religious involvement.[28] The mainliners did not want to be identified with what they determined to be the strident and hostile religious and political attitudes toward gays and lesbians in general.

Critics of both Ms. Bryant's involvement and the Protestant national leadership would point out the contradiction between denying ordination to practicing homosexual persons while going on record in support of antidiscrimination practices in the area of public housing and opportunities for employment.

A fourth factor emerged, a clear division of the house on the issue of how the Scriptures should be interpreted on matters of sodomy and homosexuality.

In The United Methodist Church, the evolution of the church's position can be charted by reference to its Social Principles statement of 1972. Appeals to that statement were made by the 1976 General Conference regarding ordination. Further appeal to the Social Principles statement, with an elaborate footnote, was made by the 1980 General Conference. At the 1984 General Conference the language became more formal and was incorporated in paragraph 402 of *The Discipline*:

> Since the practice of homosexuality is incompatible with Christian teaching, self-avowed practicing homosexuals are not to be accepted as candidates, ordained as ministers, or appointed to serve in The United Methodist Church.[29]

The 1988 General Conference elected to retain the same wording. Allowing for some variation in language within the mainline Christian denominations, the pattern is fairly clear. Churches oriented toward a hierarchical model of governance in which pastors may be appointed took a stronger stand against the ordination of the homosexuals: the Roman Catholic Church, The United Methodist Church, the Greek Orthodox Church in the U.S., the Episcopal Church. Those churches under the direct influence of Wesleyan doctrine and teaching, such as the Church of the Nazarene, the Christian and Missionary Alliance, the Wesleyan Church, also have taken a clear stand against ordination of homosexuals.[30]

The United Presbyterian Church in the U.S.A., since merged with the Presbyterian Church U.S. in 1985 to form the Presbyterian Church U.S.A., does not directly appoint ministers and operates more on a "call" basis, although not as fiercely independent as the Baptist, Mennonite, Friends, or U.C.C. groups. However, the moral and spiritual guidance to the presbyteries from the General Assembly was clearly stated in 1978 and has not been changed. Challenged at every biennial General Assembly meeting since its passage, it has not been revised to date. A similar observation can be made about the other mainline denominations. At each of the national legislative gatherings since 1978 (the watershed year), petitions and debate have focused on liberalizing the qualifications for ordination and dropping the language that in one way or another disqualifies from being ordained or retaining ordination those who declare themselves to engage in the practice of homosexuality.

Among the churches that operate on a purely call basis, such as the U.C.C. and Baptist, the national debate does not parallel the furious debate of the late 1970s in the United Presbyterian and United Methodist churches. In the case of the U.C.C., a local congregation can nominate and sponsor a person as a candidate for ordination if the candidate can persuade the congregation to do so. However, there's a catch! Unlike The United Methodist Church, and somewhat unlike the United Presbyterian Church, a U.C.C. clergy person has no guarantee that a church will call him or her as a pastor. The theological issue may be left up to the conscience of the local congregation. The practical realities take a different turn in the call-oriented denominational groups.

The authority of scripture and the conventional guidance of theology were affirmed by those who oppose the ordination of self-avowed practicing homosexuals as the basis for declaring such behavior wrong. In the churches' refinement of language, while maintaining a stance against ordination of gays and lesbians, the focus remains on a candidate's or pastor's behavior. This insistence that the behavior is the disqualifier implies that the issue is not one's orientation or the nature of one's sexual fantasies or imagery. Rather the issue is one's conduct and conduct that a person openly acknowledges and claims actively for oneself. The decisions are not based on hearsay or rumor but upon the integrity of one's statement about personal behavior. For a biblical "bottom line" basis for this argument, see chapter 5, pp. 65, 68.

The language and debate in the various denominations clarified that the issue is behavior, not orientation; it is practice, not preference; it is moral standards for clergy, not subjective feelings. The call for the highest standards of moral and ethical behavior, not cultural patterns, was utilized to govern the arguments against the ordination of homosexuals.

**2.** *Behavior Emulation.* While the debate over ministerial ordination was focused on the interpretation of scripture, a secondary but nonetheless important issue relates to the fact and perception that clergy are spiritual, moral, and social role models for parishioners in their care. Without joining a theological debate about clergy and laity, suffice it to say that part of the theological concern among laity is a clergy whose behavior is understood both by clergy and laity as a lifestyle from which at least parishioners gain admirable spiritual and moral guidance.

A. B. Simpson reminds us in his reflections on Numbers 16:9 that the tribe of Levi (the clergy) is a "separation which Christ requires and which He gives. . . . It is not the world that stains us, but the love of the world."[31] The Christian and the clergy are set apart not so much from each other but from the world. The behavior emulation is a complex issue. There are both obvious and subtle forms of behavior emulation.

At the obvious level, there may be little difference in the interpersonal skills, sensitivities, nurturance, love, tenderness, and compassion between homophiles and the general population. In fact, some of the well-founded concern both by heterosexuals and homosexuals about homophobia centers on the crude, cruel, and distorting stereotypes of homosexual mannerisms. The politically conservative or the so-called right wing traditionally has disassociated itself from homosexual affiliations. However this reality too is more complex than some think.

For example, on September 3, 1988, Associated Press wire service carried an article commenting on Utah's Senator Orrin Hatch's comment that the Democratic Party is "the party of the homosexuals." David Jones, a gay rights lobbyist at the time, had in fact once served as a fund-raiser for Hatch and in other Republican campaigns for state office. Jones produced a photograph taken on December 4, 1984 showing him with Senator Hatch at a fund-raising event. AP reports, "Jones said he doubted Hatch knew he was a homosexual at the time of the 1984 fund-raiser, 'but I think all the people I worked with were aware of it. I have lived with the same man for 20 years and have made no secret of it.' "[32]

In his book *Citizen Cohn*, Nicholas von Hoffman chronicles the life, including the homosexual behavior, of Roy Cohn, one-time chief legal counsel to anti-communist headhunter Joseph McCarthy.

> The first time Roy had been profiled on the program ["60 Minutes"] in 1979, he was at the zenith of his power, which may explain why CBS went into the tank for him. The courtly Morley Safer spoke these lines about the best-known homosexual at the top of the nation's political power pyramid: 'New York's matchmakers have given up on him. He's just not the marrying kind, though at one time, he says, he and Barbara Walters almost got married. Barbara won't comment, except to praise Roy for his loyalty.'

With reference to the biblical injunction against homosexuality (Leviticus 20:13), Von Hoffman observes:

> Roy and his political allies had fun over the years, pointing to the contradiction between the limousine liberals' wealth and where they let the heart's blood bleed, but that cleavage is as nothing compared to the one Roy had to live with throughout his adult life and which he did not address. Are there two moralities, one for himself and his friends, and one for the masses? Does power, wealth, and influence carry with it moral dispensations, does it edit out of Leviticus the words of condemnation?

Finally Von Hoffman writes:

> A distinction is sometimes made between being homosexual and being gay. (Homosexual refers to the gender of those with whom one has sex; gay refers to the folkways and fashions of the self-defined homosexual world.) Using this distinction, Roy was pronouncedly homosexual for decades, but only seldom gay. He was, however, at his most relaxed and gayest in Provincetown, a place that had taken on an aspect of Dionysian abandon by the 1970s.[33]

The tolerance and accommodation of top political power brokers not only for Roy Cohn and others is quite remarkable when the dominant public expression is one of opposition in political speeches and statements.

Christopher Hitchens has written that many gays and lesbians find public and social protection under right-wing political and religious groups. "Honesty means loss of power, so
gays on the right toe the line and gay bash. . . . There is of
course self-hatred in all this, personal but perhaps ideological."
Hitchens goes on to observe, "Yet history speaks of a long and
not so surprising connection between homosexuality and the
right. One can look to the church and the military. 'Gay' has
never necessarily meant 'left.' "[34]

The traditional behavioral stereotypes often used by conservative and right-wing religious and political groups may well be a
cover-up and a projection of their own fears and behavior. One
must exercise extreme caution in these matters, and the wisdom
of the mainline denominations about this issue is well received.

A more substantial concern is *subtle* behavioral emulation.
Here the issue shifts from the more social, public, and obvious
behaviors to those that relate to the basic nature of human
beings. In theological terms we are talking about the ontology
(nature of being) of humanity itself. Here the churches anchor
their argument substantially in the teachings of Scripture and the
theologians of the church: Augustine, Aquinas, Luther, Calvin,
Wesley, Barth, Brunner, and Tillich. The traditional theological
and scriptural position of the church as expressed by these theologians argues that heterosexuality is the ordained behavior in
creation and in covenant. A violation of this intention of creation
for our behavioral moral order is at odds with God's revelation.
This subtle and deep contradiction of homosexual behavior over
against the intention of creation would imply that homosexual
behavior is not a behavior to be emulated.


## CONCLUSION

The contemporary debate over the church's stance on homosexuality occurs along three lines of controversy. The first is the

theological one. What is the nature of being itself, God's and human beings ? The theological debate, if it is adequate, must be bipolar: It must include thoughtful discussion about the nature of God *and* about the nature of creation, including sexuality. To use theological language to present essentially psychological and sociological constructs does a disservice to the church's debate and its conclusions. The responsible discussion must have both existential and ontological components.

The second and certainly more visible controversy is the understanding of homosexuality that comes from the social sciences. The shift in American culture over the awareness and acceptance of homosexuality among a significant percentage (5 to 10 percent) of the population has been under way since the mid-forties. Especially influential was the 1948 Kinsey Report. The thrust and resolve of the civil rights movement of the 1960s spawned the gay liberation movement followed by the quest in the 1970s to ordain homosexuals in mainline denominations. The controversy has been tumultuous.

From a Christian perspective, the debate must continue in the effort to separate the social sciences issues from the theological issues. The fundamental question for the church remains: Has theology become sociology? Despite social and psychological outcries to be sensitive and compassionate toward homosexuals, what is the church's theological resolve and authority apart from social and psychological forces?

Finally, the debate of the 1970s and 1980s within the Christian churches in the United States has become a platform in which the theological/biblical and the social/psychological issues have been joined. The decision of the General Assembly of the United Presbyterian Church in May 1978 to offer its guidance to the New York presbytery has become a watershed or landmark action in Protestantism in the United States.

The controversy obviously will continue. The tension no doubt will increase between those who claim that the Scriptures are the primary authority for matters of faith and those who

look to the insights, wisdom, and counsel of the secular culture
as it sets forth its final authority in sociological and psychological terms. While the traditionalists would hold fast to the
authority of scripture, the revisionists' response is seen in the
work of Bishop John Spong who, against the counsel and sanc-
tions of the Episcopal Church, chose to ordain Roger Williams.
Likewise in the Lutheran Church, the ordination of two lesbians
and a gay man have been accomplished in San Francisco.

The conflict between the traditionalists and the revisionists,
when it comes to the practice of ordination, is on a collision
course. In the case where an unauthorized ordination has
occurred, the traditionalists have not been willing or perhaps
able to appeal to the authority of church canon and act against a
peer bishop who has performed an unauthorized ordination.
How this conflict between church law and the autonomous
actions of elected bishops will work itself out remains to be
seen. As the representative membership on the national assemblies of the various denominations continues to change its com-
position each election round (some every other year and some
every four years), it is clear that unless a huge groundswell
from the grassroots spiritual constituency of the churches
reaches beyond existing governing legislation to actually recall
or dismiss espicopal leadership for explicit failure to comply
with the will and intention of the church's theology, we can
anticipate more rather than fewer unauthorized ordinations. It
could well be that by the turn of the century, the landmark decisions of the 1970s, symbolized by the 1978 General Assembly
of the United Presbyterian Church U.S.A., will be overturned
and a new definition and understanding of the phrase "of sacred
worth" will be written both on the ecclesial books of the
Protestant churches and on the minds and in the hearts of its
constituent members.

# CHAPTER 7

# Homosexuality and
# the Church's Ministry

## Introduction

The position of this book assumes several theological truths: (1) God's intention for creating male and female human beings is for heterosexual relations. (2) The highest fulfillment of a sexual covenant is through male-and-female marriage. (3) From a theological and biblical basis, homosexual behavior is not the highest fulfillment of the human spirit. (4) Homosexual behavior is a variant or a developmental divergence from heterosexual patterns.

The principal issue for the church and its ministry lies in three barriers rising out of the church's confusion over its high calling for individual and communal life: *(a)* The church must overcome its homophobic reactions to individuals or families in which homosexuality is a matter of public knowledge. *(b)* The church must understand that homosexual behavior is not an aberrant disease; rather, it is a difference in sexual expression measured by degree not kind. *(c)* The church must show compassion toward individuals and families for whom it would seek to be a haven of refuge and hope, for rebuilding a more secure spiritual and sexual future.

In its landmark 1978 action, the United Presbyterian Church reaffirmed its 1971 support of the civil rights of homosexuals, urged the church to engage in compassionate ministry, and attempted to set aside its tendency toward homophobic reaction to homosexuality.

As recently as the 1988 General Conference of The United Methodist Church, the issue of the church's theological stand on its ministry to homosexuals is reflected in the adoption of paragraph 71.F in *The Book of Discipline* (1988). Words added by the 1988 General Conference appear in boldface type:

> Homosexual persons no less than heterosexual persons are individuals of sacred worth. All persons need the ministry and guidance of the Church in their struggles for human fulfillment, as well as the spiritual and emotional care of a fellowship which enables reconciling relationships with God, with others, and with self. Although we do not condone the practice of homosexuality and consider this practice incompatible with Christian teaching, **we affirm that God's grace is available to all. We commit ourselves to be in ministry for and with all persons.**

The strategies of both these mainline denominations indicate the church is more effectively hearing its call to be in ministry to the homosexual community.

### Individuals

In an article in *Moody Monthly,* Darlene Bogle reports on her experience. Having been a sexually active lesbian for five years, she wandered into a church in California and eventually made an appointment with the pastor to seek prayerful support for her effort to go straight.

> After several minutes of small talk, I blurted out that I'd been involved in homosexual activity and asked for his counsel and prayer as I sought to break ties with my past. He drew back his broad shoulders and stiffened his padded black leather chair. His words shattered my fragile spirit. "I'll certainly pray for you, Darlene," he said, "but in 23 years of ministry, I've never yet seen a homosexual change for any prolonged period."[1]

Bogle goes on to describe her struggles with her own homosexuality and with pastors and churches who endeavored to help her through a twelve-year struggle to "know full deliverance from homosexual bondage."

Dan Roberts of Quest Learning Center in Reading, Pennsylvania, is quoted as saying, "Telling a gay person to 'quit' is like telling a hungry person not to be hungry."[2] British psychologist Elizabeth Moberly has taken a position that is both compassionate and empathetic in efforts to help people who want to change. In *Homosexuality: A New Christian Ethic,* she writes, "It will take the view that a homosexual orientation does not depend on a genetic predisposition, hormonal imbalance, or abnormal learning processes, but on difficulties in the parent-child relationship, especially in the earlier years of life."[3] Pushing the church further toward ministry, Moberly argues that the church has failed to provide most what it promises to all, including homosexuals, that is, a context within which to develop nonsexual, same-sex relationships.

Initially, the attitude of the church needs to be one of *acceptance of the sacred worth* of gay men and lesbians. Here we are talking about a person's being and potential, not just one's current relationship, feelings, or attitudes. Therefore, the first gesture of offering ministry to homosexuals is to step through the veils of homophobia, moral righteousness, and personal fear coupled to biblical and psychological proof-texting.

The more theologically conservative one is, the more likely one is to fall into the trap of believing that if a homosexual undergoes a "born again" Christian conversion experience, this automatically brings about a change in sexual behavior and sexual orientation from homosexual to heterosexual. The conversion experience is seen as a repenting of the sinfulness of life— and of those sins cataloged in the Scriptures, both Old and New. Homosexuality is but *one* of many human conditions and activities that result from the Fall. For some persons an instantaneous conversion may result in total personal transformation.

For most however, the sins of the heart require a longer period of nurture in a loving Christian community to lose force. In ministering to individual homosexuals, the church needs to be cautious about demanding from individuals more than what the church asks of itself or its leaders: A willingness to acknowledge and confess sins does not remove the source of temptation or produce instantaneous deliverance.

The church and its members need to be positive *role models* to the homosexual community. Positive role models are formed out of consistent, positive behavior and not sharp moralisms. The key initial dynamic informing any kind of trusting relationship is developing an attitude of acceptance and confidence. This is true in counseling; in sales work; in evangelism; in the ministry of the church. Being compassionate toward someone cannot be confused with total acceptance of a person's behavior and lifestyle. But theological and spiritual rejection of a lifestyle or set of behaviors dare not be so abusive, harsh, or condemnatory that "moral correctives" preclude the development of any kind of relationship in which "tough compassion" (a loving relationship in which high expectations of accountability to transcendent moral norms are expected of all participants) is possible. Without tough compassion, the fulfillment of ministry cannot occur.

Dr. C. Philip Hinerman said it well several years ago:

> So I am very weary of the irony in this debate. I am weary of the stereotype of the liberal who in his support for the homosexual lifestyle is considered "compassionate," even as he rejects what are for me the clear words of Scripture condemning this aberration. Perhaps what is needed in this debate more than anything else is a new breed of Christian men and women who are in tune with their own divided sexual drives, and who are aware of their own sexual weaknesses, whatever the weakness may be. Perhaps we need a new breed of Christian men and women who are also committed to a lifestyle free of that which the Bible condemns as sexual sin, whether that be homosexual sin or heterosexual sin.[4]

One must be impressed by the tough compassion of Dr. Hinerman toward the entire church community since this statement predated the sexual aberrations of both Jim Bakker and Jimmy Swaggart. Unless the attitude of tough compassion is consistently expressed, the church will fail in its intended efforts, and those identified with the gay and/or lesbian community will become even further embittered and distrusting of the moralistic and homophobic harshness of the church. Heterosexual Christians owe themselves and their companions in creation a more compassionate response.

### Families

**1.** *Shock/Embarrassment/Denial.* Beyond the tough compassion needed for the church's ministry among individual homosexuals, perhaps the wider and more important and enduring ministry is to the families of homosexuals. Since the late 1940s, the "family systems" approach to counseling has become more and more important in counseling and psychotherapy. The basic assumption is that while one member of a family may be the "identified patient," the "black sheep," the "scapegoat," or the "trouble-maker," the real problem is the entire family's system and not just the weak link. A whole body of literature on family systems theory treats the family as a whole unit. To disturb or change one aspect or component of that family system is inevitably to alter, disrupt, and change the entire family. The change may not always be obvious or acknowledged, but if one part of the system is changed, it affects all other parts.

The family is immensely important in the developmental stability of any individual member. Currently nearly half of all marriages end in divorce, and projections suggest that by 1992 nearly 60 percent of all children under the age of eighteen will have spent a portion of their lives in a single-parent family. The marital problems, coupled with the obvious statistical realities relating to divorces, custody settlements, single parents, and stepchildren within the church, reveal the multiplicity of problems that surround remarriages, "married-again Christians," or "blended families." We have many clear indicators that our family systems require more than human resources can furnish.

Therefore the church has a ministry to *all* its families, including—perhaps especially—to the families in which either a parent or a child has mustered the courage to disclose his or her homosexuality. Many Christians deeply yearn for a tough compassion from their churches. Unlike the insensitive and homophobic pastors poignantly described by Darlene Bogle at the beginning of this chapter, the church family needs to overcome its own shock, embarrassment, and denial in order to be of ministerial assistance to families in which homosexuality has become a manifest issue.

From a counseling or therapeutic point of view, the least helpful type of response the church can make is to reinforce the "black sheep," "scapegoat," or "identified patient" syndrome which displaces and distorts the real issue. In so doing the church would destroy the subtle and powerful infrastructure of the family, which needs rejuvenation and new strength to deal with its problems. The problem is never isolated in the obvious and identified family member. The problems are always deeper and more systemic than the crises seen in the hospital emergency room, the courthouse, the jail, the pastor's study, or the school counselor's office. The church has a responsibility to restrain itself from simplistic responses both to others' needs and to its own insecurity as a wish to make problems (especially those relating to homosexuality) disappear.

From a pastoral therapeutic perspective, John Fortunato advances the argument that change for the homosexual person is not possible. He claims that homosexuality continues into adult years, with an emotional and physical attraction to the same sex. The struggle for the church, for the families, for the individuals involved in homosexuality is not easy.[5] Unless the church can extend its ministry with deep and calm confidence to families that are subsets of God's family—the household of

God—human families will founder in their efforts to help family members struggling with the issues of homosexuality.

The church must minister to its whole family with a system capable of nurture and discerning moral judgment, of loving and correcting, of caring and confronting, of empathy and contradiction, of acceptance and directing. If the household of God is to minister well and effectively, it must minister where needs exist, including the dilemma of homosexual and heterosexual members of the same family.

In an address to the Council of Bishops of The United Methodist Church, Bishop Earl Hunt said, "This [homosexual] community's men and women are 'individuals of sacred worth'[6] for whom a Saviour died." Bishop Hunt continues:

> Let it be said emphatically that the problem of homophobia, morally reprehensible and pragmatically serious, must be addressed far more effectively by the Christian community than has been done up until now. *Positive* efforts to offer pastoral care to homosexual people and to make clear to them the unqualified love and concern promised in *The Book of Discipline* must become an intentional part of United Methodism's program in ministry on all levels. However, the acceptance of homosexuality as a lifestyle compatible with Christianity is *not* required in order to oppose homophobia.[7]

Whether one is Presbyterian, United Methodist, Baptist, Pentecostal, Roman Catholic—or whether one's familial ties are within the Christian family—the affirmation that all people are of sacred worth can be an effective rallying point to call the church into effective, consistent, conscientious help that is directed to families in which homosexuality has emerged.

**2.** *The AIDS Issue.* Theologically speaking, HIV/AIDS is also an important aspect of the church's ministry to its entire community, homosexual as well as heterosexual. AIDS is *not* essentially a homosexual issue. We dare not continue to identify AIDS solely as a homosexual disease.

AIDS is a very serious medical and epidemiological problem. It is also an appropriate cause for Christian concern. AIDS should be addressed because it is a problem that plagues both the homosexual and heterosexual communities—indeed, human life itself. The church must avoid the stance that the "good," or "straight" Christians are called to engage in ministry to the "less fortunate" afflicted with AIDS. HIV/AIDS is a public health issue for all. It is a major theological problem because it confronts the Christian church as a human problem, not because it is a sexual problem. The church must make a practical and moral response. In an article in *The Christian Century,* Ronald J. Sider speaks to the church's role in the AIDS crisis.[8] He advocates four essential tasks for the church. First, the church needs to set a good example by not fearing casual contact with homosexuals in its ministries, since it is clearly demonstrated that casual contact does not spread HIV/AIDS.

Second, Sider suggests that the church needs to be directly and actively involved in pastoral counseling services and other means of ministry. The work of ministers like Earl Shelp and Ronald Sunderland along with Peter Mansell in their book *AIDS: Personal Stories in Pastoral Perspective,* indicates ways in which the church should and can be directly involved in providing ministry to the people with AIDS in their families.[9]

A third way, suggests Sider, is education. He points out that the church is essentially a trusted institution within the community and should engage in the type of educational role that I suggested earlier. Currently no vaccine or preventative for AIDS exists. Therefore education is a ministry of the church. Shelp and Sunderland's *Handle with Care* shows congregations how to organize care teams of laypeople who help with social, emotional, spiritual, and physical challenges faced by people living with AIDS.[10]

Fourth, Sider believes the church should follow along the lines suggested by this study and others that theological reflection on the issues of AIDS is needed. Sider comments, "Those four points take only three minutes to articulate, to incarnate them requires a lifetime of struggle."[11]

In addition to the kinds of assistance suggested by Sider, or Shelp, Sunderland, and Mansell, Father Carl Meirose of Chicago's AIDS Pastoral Care Network recommends very simple practices such as praying directly for and with people with AIDS; watching one's language to refer to "persons with AIDS" rather than "AIDS victims" and avoiding using phrases like "dying with AIDS." Ultimately, what does ministry to those with AIDS require? One Chicago man with AIDS answered, "A hug once in awhile would be nice."[12]

## Related Theological Issues

In *Habits of the Heart: Individualism and Commitment in American Life,* Robert N. Bellah and his co-authors discuss the ways that our harsh commitment to individualism is reflected in a selfish, narcissistic and self-centered lifestyle.[13] The extent to which Bellah and his fellow researchers catch us at a point of theological and cultural vulnerability is nowhere illustrated more profoundly than in the church's struggle both with AIDS and with homosexuality. *Habits of the Heart* reminds us of the difficulty of any effort to move the church in the United States beyond selfishness to offer a ministry to homosexuals and persons with AIDS. Such a ministry calls for renewed communal and corporate commitment on the part of the church. "Habits of the heart" and "homosexual lifestyle" are two challenges directly confronting the church's ministry. The church is called to offer tough compassion, a sensitive reaching-out ministry, through the local congregation to the families living with AIDS. The church is called to step beyond its own boundaries of sexual, cultural, and biological fears and arrogance.

For many ministers, however, this is a very complicated and conflicting call to ministry. Most pastors are very nurturing, accepting, and emotionally sensitive people. Because of pastors' heightened sense of caring and sensitivity, the emotional components of being a heterosexual do not have guaranteed boundaries. For example, a male pastor may have developed a very caring, compassionate attitude and feelings toward a teenage boy suffering from cancer, or toward a middle-aged male who was severely injured in a work-related accident, or toward an elderly man in deep grief over the death of his wife of forty-five years. The emotions and sensitivities elicited in these acts of pastoral care do not conform to the male macho image that only women, children, or male sissies cry or care publicly and deeply, especially toward other men. Such expressions of tenderness and empathetic concern by a male pastor may also become a source of confusion and uncertainty about his sexual identity. Emotional expressions of this nature, while applauded in a certain aspect of ministry, may become sources of ambivalence about the pastor's "true" sexual identity.

Where such confusion and uncertainty continue unresolved over a period of time, the pastor may "defend" against such stirrings in one of two ways: (1) over-identifying with a male, macho, anti-gay or lesbian ideology and display of typical homophobic language and actions; or (2) over-identifying with the gay and lesbian community as the alternative means of attempting to resolve his own ambivalence about his sexual identity. A similar dynamic would apply to female pastors, their highly nurturing skills and susceptibility to role confusion over true sexual identity.

As a consequence of the above dynamic, many potential ministries of the church toward gays and lesbians meet with a frustrating end. The pastor may suppress any gestures of ministry toward gays and lesbians and their families because the pastor's own sexuality is too threatened, and laypeople typically will not engage in prophetic ministry so volatile without the support of the clergy. If the pastor does choose to support the "gay rights" or "ordination of homosexuals" movements, unless the congregation feels the same pull or is very secure in its sexual identity, the laity will resist active, public ministries among gays and lesbians.

The process of releasing and empowering the church (clergy and laity) for active ministry among the homosexual community is more subtle than simply shedding the epithet of being a homophobic congregation. The crosscurrents of sexual uncertainties that surround and attend acts of nurture, love, and support in the church's ministry become more highly charged ambivalences when direct involvement in sexual issues, like homosexuality, presents itself. But such conflicts should not and indeed dare not prevent the church from engaging effectively in ministry toward and among those whose lives are most directly affected by gay and lesbian concerns.

A complicating factor beyond sexual identity confusion affecting a readiness for ministry is a congregation's or a denomination's theological perspective. As Christians we are called to live out the ideals of Christian life exemplified in Jesus Christ. But none of us lives out the ideal lifestyle. In everyday Christian life we all fall short of the glory of God and live out our faith somewhere between perfection and zero. Therefore, whether for gay and lesbian or heterosexual persons, the church cannot claim that one group lives the perfect life and the other is totally worthless. A congregation or pastor may hold the view, as I have suggested in this book, that many persons have predispositions for all kinds of behavior (alcoholism, depression, homosexuality), but a predisposition is not license to act. While one may maintain that one must acknowledge and maintain a distinction between *thoughts* and *acts*, the church dare not dismiss a claimed predisposition toward homosexual acts as strictly analogous to alcoholism, violence, or depression. In homosexual attraction the focus is affection, intimacy, vulnerability, and basic human relationships of warmth, nurture, and acceptance. One can live without ever drinking or smoking again; one can become less depressed or violent, or subject to radical mood shifts by taking certain medications; one can adopt new eating, work, sports, sleep, intimacy behaviors to counter the destructive forces of anorexia and bulimia, "workaholic," "sportsaholic," or misogynist lifestyles—and not be denied love, acceptance, and nurture as a human being.

If a congregation or pastor desires to minister to gays and lesbians, the beginning of help cannot be analogous to AA or Overeaters Anonymous (OA) or misogynist or abuse control. The church that endeavors to offer a nurturing community for the homosexual struggling to achieve intimacy, warmth, and acceptance will have to begin by acknowledging that none of us lives the ideal life when it comes to nurture and acceptance. The church will have to develop more subtle models for offering acceptance to the gay or lesbian who wants to live the Christian life than importing the AA model that would require the withdrawal of all emotional support.

The ministry of compassion to the homosexual community is very difficult from the perspective of the traditional (straight) church community. At one and the same time, the church acknowledges the "sacred worth" of each human being—and each person's needs for affection and acceptance—and lovingly offers a similar *affectional* lifestyle but a different *sexual* lifestyle to the homosexual. There are no other models except that of Christ that will steer the church along its course of ministry to the gay and lesbian community. The words to use are not clear, the model to offer is not obvious, the best means of offering and encouraging affection and intimacy is not transparent. But ministering to one another in our less-than-ideal Christian life as heterosexuals and homosexuals is a gift of God's grace for all because we all are of sacred worth.

Speaking out is not easy. Acting in ministry is not easy. To hold moral conviction and act with compassionate ministry is to swim against the cultural tide of individualism *and* of sexuality.[14] A variety of organizations offer resources and services to the gay community. A partial list follows. Workers at these centers would welcome contact from church groups for literature, education, opportunities to speak, and ways of guiding or assisting local churches in developing effective ministry to the gay community.

## Organizations Offering Resources/Services

Affirmation: United Methodists for Lesbian/Gay Concerns
P.O. Box 1021
Evanston, Illinois 60201
(312) 475-0499

Seeks to affirm presences and provide ministry for all individuals in The United Methodist Church community regardless of race class, age, sex, or sexual orientation.

Catholic Coalition for Gay Civil Rights
c/o New Ways Ministry
4012 29th Street
Mt. Rainier, MD 20822
(301) 277-5674

Courage
c/o St. Michael's Rectory
424 W. 34th Street
New York, NY 10001
(212) 421-0426

Functions as a spiritual support group for homosexuals who want to live by teachings of Catholicism. Encourages members to give up homosexual lifestyles in favor of celibacy sustained by prayer, meetings, and development of chaste relationships.

Dignity, Inc.
1500 Massachusetts Avenue, N.W. Suite 11
Washington, DC 20005
(202) 861-0017

Believes that gay and lesbian Catholics are members of Christ's mystical body numbered among people of God, and that it is the right, duty, and privilege of gay or lesbian persons to live the sacramental life of the church.

Evangelicals Concerned
c/o Dr. Ralph Blair
311 E. 72nd St., No. G-1
New York, NY 10021
(212) 517-3171

Task Force founded by the National Association of Evangelicals. Christian homosexuals and heterosexuals concerned with "lack of preparation for dealing realistically with homosexuals in evangelical communities and the implications of the Gospel in the lives of gay men and lesbians."

Exodus International—North America
P.O. Box 2121
San Rafael, CA 94912
(415) 454-1017

Exodus is a coordinating agency that offers more than seventy ministries to help people leaving the homosexual lifestyle. "Central to Exodus' purpose is equipping the body of Christ, in its various forms, to minister to the homosexual."

Life
P.O. Box 353
New York, NY 10185
(212) 967-4828

Nondenominational Christian mission seeking to help homosexuals who want to overcome their "mental and emotional bondage."

National Center for Gay Ministry
4012 29th St.
Mt. Rainer, MD 20822
(301) 277-5674

New Ways Ministry
4012 29th Street
Mt. Rainier, MD 20712
(301) 277-5674

Attempts to provide adequate and accurate information in the

Roman Catholic Church and society. Promotes theological dialogue, describes and promotes gay civil rights.

Parents & Friends of Lesbians & Gays
P.O. Box 27605
Washington, DC 20038
(202) 628-5331

Pride Institute
1400 Martin Dr.
Eden Prairie, MN 55344
(612) 934-7554

An alcohol treatment center for gays and lesbians.

Reconciling Congregations Program
P.O. Box 23636
Washington, DC 20005
(202) 863-1586

United Methodist congregations seeking to affirm the participation of gay and lesbian members in church affairs and to resolve differences and problems between The United Methodist Church and homosexuals in the United States.

Transforming Congregations
c/o The Rev. Robert Kuyper
Trinity United Methodist Church
724 Niles St.
Bakersfield, CA 93305
(805) 325-0785

Transforming Congregations is an informal network of Christian congregations that provides resources for study of the issues of homosexuality *and* stands ready to welcome those persons already struggling with a gay or lesbian lifestyle into their congregational life.

Universal Fellowship of Metropolitan Community Churches
5300 Santa Monica Blvd., Suite 304
Los Angeles, CA 90029
(213) 464-5100

Christian group ministering to homosexual communities through worship and social action.

# CHAPTER 8

# Intimacy, Vulnerability, and Sexuality

## Introduction

As an effort to summarize this book, we need to embrace the theological and psychological claim that we are sexual beings. To be human is to be sexual. We are created that way. God loves us that way. We are created to love each other that way. And that love is best expressed and divinely called to be demonstrated in the male/female, heterosexual relationship. The covenant relationship in which our sexuality is most fully expressed is heterosexual marriage. Without exception in both biblical times and times throughout the life of the church, individuals of sacred worth have given their lives to celibacy as a long-term commitment. In the Roman Catholic tradition celibacy is understood as an act of sacrificial ministry.

As suggested in chapter 2, Sigmund Freud provides rich insights into the nature of human sexuality.[1] He argued for the bisexuality of the human being. How that sexuality is learned, expressed, given and received in appropriate and effective ways depends in large measure on the family, society, and the life and the ministry of the church. The intention for the created order is for heterosexual relationships, but we are not created with a predetermined biological guarantee of how to act sexually. If such a protection or guarantee were part of human nature, human beings would not have received "the breath of life" (Genesis 2).

Human sexuality is very much what we make out of the

breath of life given us. There are no psychological or theological guarantees. Humans have no crippling shackles either. Rather, like it or not, human life is a lifelong struggle to achieve appropriate sexual expression that may be summarized as the three categories of *intimacy, vulnerability,* and *sexual acts.*

## Intimacy

The notion of intimacy suggests a social, spiritual, and individual sensitivity, closeness, mutual nurture, that goes far beyond the sense of "intimacy" as a euphemism for sexual intercourse. One may be intimate with another while engaged in the act of sexual intercourse. But the word *intimacy,* at its higher level, refers to the spiritual intimacy/spiritual union with God or the emotional intimacy/bonding with our fellow human beings. Intellectual intimacies with the ideas and thoughts that empower us, biological intimacy in terms of the closeness and comfortableness we have with our own bodies, and the sexual intimacy of close physical, intellectual, emotional, and spiritual intimacy—*all* are expressions of intimacy.

In *Sex with Confidence,* I have stated, "Without intimacy there's a tendency for fear, anxiety, and suspicion to run rampant. . . . Intimacy, in contrast, provides a framework in which genuine sexual freedom and fun can flourish. Intimacy is a safe playground where the spice and surprises of healthy sex can be enjoyed to the fullest. There is, indeed, a kind of sexual magic that accompanies true intimacy. But to make the most of that magic, you've got to see the bedroom as a part of much larger, all-encompassing bond of love."[2]

## Vulnerability

One can espouse the virtues of mutuality, self-giving, *agape* love, warm and affectionate relationships. The wide variety of behaviors suggested by these terms, as positive as they all seem, are behaviors and attitudes that flow from the fountain-head that makes intimacy possible.

Unless we are willing to let ourselves be *vulnerable,* mutuality, warmth, affection, even the intellectual idea of *agape* love are all guarded guises by which we avoid plunging into true intimacy. Vulnerability is a means by which we take the plunge. Experiencing vulnerability is like jumping from the high dive into a chilly swimming pool. Once the leap of vulnerability occurs, there is no turning back. You are committed! As suggested by Bellah in *Habits of the Heart,* ours is an age and a culture committed to individualism and not to community. For commitment to be genuine, we must engage our vulnerability. To make a commitment to another is to be self-exposed, vulnerable, and open for exploitation, abuse, rejection, and failure. M. Scott Peck in *The Road Less Traveled* urges us toward love that is a commitment to spiritual, emotional, social vulnerability.[3]

Too many of us have experienced rejection, failure, abuse, embarrassment, and negative responses. We become the "muppets" of Bellah's study. We retreat into individualism. For intimacy to flourish, vulnerability must first be offered. Someone has to break the bondage. One partner has to break the impasse. Somebody has to break the barriers of hostility, fear, self-protection, and self-righteousness. One individual in a marriage relationship, or in a family, or in a ministry to homosexuals must have the courage to take the lead of being vulnerable in love.

Having taken the first steps of vulnerability, how does one relate to a partner, family member, or a person in the gay or lesbian community whose sexual preference for same-sex partners may make them frightening or threatening in our eyes? My call for a willingness by heterosexuals to be vulnerable and open to gay and lesbian individuals has a twofold purpose: (1) Whether our gender is male or female, each person carries aspects of the opposite sex and therefore no one is completely, 100 percent male or female. If one restricts feelings of warmth, acceptance, and nurture to gender opposites, a part of one's personhood is

denied. Being vulnerable as a heterosexual socially and spiritually to the life and experience of gays and lesbians is an invitation to the heterosexual to be more open to the emotions of
love, warmth, and acceptance that make all human relations
more genuine. For the heterosexual the invitation to emotional
vulnerability is to be less afraid and denying of the broad range
of human emotions that each person is capable of developing
and expressing in appropriate gestures of affection and acceptance. (2) Heterosexuals need more social, intellectual, and
spiritual exposure to the homosexual community so that com-
munication and friendship might be possible. If, as I maintain
in this book, homosexual behavior is essentially a function of
human development circumstances, then heterosexuals are
called by this invitation to vulnerability to act with loving grace
toward those whose sexual identity has taken a different developmental track. The goal of vulnerability is not simply taking
the first step and being emotionally exposed by a willingness to
experience rejection and failure. The goal of vulnerability is a
statement that "I am willing to run the high risk of embarrassment and rejection in order to relate to you."

An intimate relationship begins as one reaches into the life of
another—an individual, a family, Sunday school class, a small
group discussion in a gay community. The leap of faith of vulnerability is the risk of offering one's presence and personhood
to engage in the level of discourse and intimacy the other is
willing to risk. The first step is the vulnerability required to
develop the character of, increase the security system of, and to
offer tough compassion toward others.

The vulnerability factor is a twofold experience. First is the
willingness of the initiator to go through the rejection and
embarrassment of being considered silly, stupid, or unworthy.
Second, and the more intentional and complicated aspect of
vulnerability, is the long-suffering, patient attitude of endeavor-
ing to create, build, and strengthen the character of "the other."
As the other feels more secure, one's vulnerability becomes less

threatening and more of an invitation. The less one is threatened by the rejection from the other, the more one is willing to be vulnerable. Gradually the other begins to feel more secure and more capable of being vulnerable himself or herself.

As that process continues, we have the emergence of what Harry Stack Sullivan referred to as the *state of love*: "When satisfaction or the security of another person becomes as significant to one as is one's own satisfaction or security, then the state of love exists."[4] The emergence of love is the flower of intimacy, nurtured by the taproot of vulnerability. When one is able to engage in the twofold process of vulnerability and receive gestures and acts of vulnerability on the part of another, true intimacy occurs. This creative vulnerability feeds love, nurtures true mutuality, and blossoms into intimacy.

### Sexual Acts

We are all sexual beings, and sexual acts are but one manifestation of our being. They neither create nor are a derivative of intimacy or vulnerability. Abusive behavior, incest, rape (violent and public or quiet bedroom rape) are experiences or expressions of sexual acts that have not been grafted into the flower of vulnerability and intimacy. At the time of creation (Genesis 1 and 2), God expressed God's self in the vulnerability and intimacy woven into all of creation. There is an intimate and vulnerable way in which God broods over the waters and gently separates day from night, pushes trees into blossom, sends fishes of the sea scurrying, animals of the land lumbering, cumbersome feathered wings soaring.

In the creation story no mention of sexuality is suggested until Adam and Eve appear. The pinnacle of creation is the spiritually equal creation man and woman, male and female. The blessing and invitation "Be fruitful and multiply" is an invitation certainly to engage in heterosexual acts. Heterosexual acts become the grafting-in process of the mutuality that keeps men and women from lapsing into Robert Bellah's narcissistic individualism. Beyond the obvious suggestion of bearing children, we can conclude that God's invitation *and* admonition is the crowning act of creation. Adam and Eve were encouraged not only to engage in biological multiplication but also to use the breath of life of vulnerability and intimacy to nurture those relationships that give honor and glory to maleness and femaleness and to humanity's relationship with God.

The penultimate sexual satisfactions as attested by the gay and lesbian community—including those who understand themselves to be gay and lesbian Christians—is the mutuality, intimacy, and sensitivity that, however intense, personal, and satisfying it might be, falls short of the full potential of human sexuality as ordained by God and revealed in the Bible to be marriage between a man and a woman. That full potential is discovered—however poignantly, painfully, and creatively—not in same-sex intimacy and mutuality but in opposite-sex mutuality, vulnerability, and intimacy.

The dipolar nature of deity and creation, male and female, person and community, church and society, individual and family, is extended to and inclusive of the oppositional forces of life. When we reflect upon the truly dipolar nature of life, we understand that we are called to offer vulnerability and intimacy to same-sex persons, whether peers, parents, or children, but the highest and most profound expression of vulnerability and intimacy among human beings occurs in the interaction of male and female.

The paradigm given us in creation includes sexual acts as well as social, spiritual, emotional, and intellectual acts. The gift of creation is its fundamental dipolarity. Intimacy and caring flow from a vulnerability that is always uncertain and unsettled because vulnerability with one who is opposite—in gender, space, creation, and biology—is an impetus toward growth.

In understanding and receiving the powerful forces of opposites in male and female relations, we learn the paradigm and the pattern for the opposites of human beings and God. That vulnerability and that intimacy do not come from human initiative. They come from the very act of creation itself by which God gives us the breath of life as the potential to enter fully, effectively, and intimately into love in genuinely oppositional and complementary relationships. The highest form of these relationships in human terms is husband and wife, male and female. The highest form of these relationships in spiritual terms is our relationship with God. The divine initiative of God woos us by the prevenient grace of the Holy Spirit and is manifest in God's love for us in Jesus Christ.

## CONCLUSION

This study endeavors to show that reading of scripture, reflection upon the theological witness to scripture, the insights and understandings that we gain from modern psychology, pastoral care, and the nature of the church all argue that heterosexuality is normative. The underlying assumption in this study is that the Bible is the final authority for teaching and life of the Christian. The Bible is a book about God and faith, not primarily about sexual morality. The invitation of the Scriptures and the church is to the highest and deepest level of intimacy and vulnerability with God. Such intimacy is not possible without the sexual self-acceptance of oneself as male or female and the creative dipolar mutuality that achieves its highest human expression in heterosexual relationships.

# NOTES

## 1. We Are Sexual Beings

1. This is an excerpt from a letter (March 6, 1956) written by Lewis to a Mr. Masson and may be seen in the Wade Collection, Wheaton College, Wheaton, Ill. Portions of the letter appear in *The Broken Image* by Leanne Payne (Westchester, Ill.: Crossway Books, 1981), 91, 92.
2. James Wall, "Editorials," *The Christian Century* (August 13-20, 1986), 700.
3. *See* James B. Nelson, "Sexuality, Christian Theology and Ethics of" in *Dictionary of Pastoral Care and Counseling,* ed. Rodney J. Hunter (Nashville: Abingdon Press, 1990), 1156.
4. Norman Pittenger, *Unbounded Love: God and Man in Process* (New York: Seabury Press, 1976), 18.
5. James B. Nelson, *Embodiment* (Minneapolis: Augsburg Publishing House, 1978), 33.
6. John Leo, "What Qualifies as Sexual Harassment?" *U.S. News & World Report* (August 13, 1990), 17.
7. Clarence Petersen, "For this group, chastity is the route to lasting love," *Chicago Tribune* as reprinted in *The Durham Morning Herald* (August 21, 1988), 2E.

## 2. The Purpose Of Sexuality Is Intimacy

1. R. Stephen Warner, "The Metropolitan Community Church as a Case Study of Religious Change in the U.S.A." (paper presented to the Society for the Scientific Study of Religion, Salt Lake City, October 1989), 34-36.
2. W. G. Herron *et al.*,"New Psychoanalytic Perspectives on the Treatment of a Homosexual Male," *Journal of Homosexuality* 5 (Summer 1980), 396-97.
3. Charles W. Socarides, "Homosexuality is not Just an Alternative Life Style," in *Male and Female: Christian Approaches to Sexuality,* ed. R. Barnhouse and U. Holmes (New York: Seabury Press, 1976), 146. Italics are mine.
4. Jay Greenburg and Stephen Mitchell, *Object Relations in Psychoanalytic Theory* (Cambridge, MA: Harvard University Press, 1983), Introduction, Chapter 1.
5. Catherine Keller, *From a Broken Web* (Boston: Beacon Press, 1986), 39. Chapters 1 and 3 expand upon this theme and heritage in illuminating ways.
6. Ibid., 33, 26.
7. James Nelson, "Men and Body Life," a paper read to the Post Patriarchal Male Sexuality Conference, Center for Process Studies, Claremont, Calif. March 30, 1990, 2-3.
8. John J. McNeill, *The Church and the Homosexual* (Kansas City: Sheed, Andrews and McMeel, 1976), 1-25.

9. *See* Norman Pittenger, *Unbounded Love* (New York: Seabury Press, 1976); *The Meaning of Being Human* (New York: The Pilgrim Press, 1982); *Time for Consent* (London: SCM Press, Ltd., 1970); and *Gay Lifestyles: A Christian Interpretation of Homosexuality and the Homosexual* (Los Angeles: Universal Fellowship Press, 1977). *Also see* D. S. Bailey, *Homosexuality and the Western Christian Tradition* (New York: Longmans, Green and Co., 1955), Introduction, pp. vii-xii, and Conclusion, 153-76.

10. McNeill, *Church and the Homosexual,* 104, 106.

11. Steven Reid, "Biblical Scholar Tells UM Women's Role Agency that Prejudice Against 'Gays,' 'Lesbians,' is Outdated", in *United Methodist Reporter,* 132:41 *(*March 14, 1986).

12. W. George McAdoo, Jr., and Louise Behrens Apperson, "Parental Factors in the Childhood of Homosexuals, in *Journal of Abnormal Psychology* 73 (3): 201, 205, 206. *See also* Irving Bieber *et al., Homosexuality: A Psychoanalytic Study* (New York: Basic Books, 1962).

13. Barbara Zanotti, in *Homosexuality and the Catholic Church,* ed. Jeannine Gramick. (Chicago: Thomas More, 1983), 82, 83.

14. James Harrison, "The Dynamics of Sexual Anxiety," *Christianity and Crisis* 37 (9, 10) (May and June 30, 1977), 137.

15. Luise J. Zucker, "Mental Health and Homosexuality," in *The Journal of Sex Research* 2 (2) (July 1966), 111-25; Sandor Rado, "A Critical Examination of the Concept of Bisexuality," in *Psychoanalytic Medicine* 2 (1940), 459-67.

16. W. G. Herron *et al.,* "New Psychoanalytic Perspectives," 398, 399, 400.

17. 16. Paul L. Lehmann, *Ethics in a Christian Context* (New York: Harper and Row, 1963), 101.

### 3. Heterosexual and Homosexual Lifestyles

1. John Calvin, *Institutes of the Christian Religion,* ed. John T. McNeill trans. Ford Lewis Battles, vol. XX. *The Library of Christian Classics* (Philadelphia: Westminster Press, 1960), 35-39.

2. Paul K. Jewett, *Man as Male and Female* (Grand Rapids: Eerdmans, 1975), 94-105.

3. Tom Horner, *Jonathan Loved David: Homosexuality in Biblical Times* (Philadelphia: Westminster Press, 1978), 20, 25, 24.

4. Ibid., 26-44, 117 ff.

### 4. The Old Testament and Homosexuality

1. Don Williams, *The Bond That Breaks: Will Homosexuality Split the Church?* (Los Angeles: BIM, 1978), 56, 57.

2. Victor Paul Furnish, *The Moral Teaching of Paul* (Nashville: Abingdon, 1979), 53, 54.

3. D. S. Bailey, *Homosexuality in the Western Christian Tradition* (London: Longmans, Green and Company, 1955).

4. John J. McNeill, *The Church and the Homosexual* (Kansas City: Sheed Andrews and McMeel, 1976).

5. Bailey, *Homosexuality,* 4, 2-3. Bailey argues, "Is it not possible that Lot, either in ignorance or in defiance of the laws of Sodom, had exceeded the rights of a *gēr* in that city by receiving and entertaining two 'foreigners' whose intentions might be hostile, and whose credentials, it seems, had not been examined? This

would afford a natural and satisfactory reason for the investment of Lot's house by the citizens, and for their demand: 'Where are the men which came in to thee this night? Bring them out unto us, that we may know them'—that is, take cognizance of them, and enquire into their *bona fides*. Lot's plea—the plea of a good host—is then perfectly intelligible: '. . . do not so wickedly . . . unto these men do nothing'—in other words: 'Since I have, rightly or wrongly, taken these strangers under my roof, do not now flout the obligation of hospitality by this unseemly demonstration . . . take no action against my guests, for they are yours also.''

6. Ibid., 10.
7. Robert Treese, "Homosexuality: A Contemporary View of the Biblical Perspective," in *Loving Women, Loving Men,* ed. S. M. Gearhart and W. R. Johnson (San Francisco: Glide, 1974), 33.
8. Henri J. M. Nouwen, *Intimacy: Pastoral Psychological Essays,* (Notre Dame: Fides Publishers, 1969), 38-52, 43. *Also see* S. J. Ridderbosch, *De Homosexuele Naaste* (ed. Janse de Jonge, Baarn: 1961).
9. Furnish, *Moral Teaching,* 56-58.
10. Williams, *Bond That Breaks,* 68, 69. *See* Gerhard Von Rad, *Genesis,* trans. John H. Marks (Philadelphia: Westminster, 1961), 213; John Gray, *Joshua, Judges, and Ruth* (London: Nelson, 1967), 632; Robert Boling, *Judges* (New York: Doubleday, 1975), 279.
11. Bailey, *Homosexuality,* 54.
12. Walther Eichrodt, *Theology of the Old Testament,* vol. I, trans. J. A. Baker (Philadelphia: Westminster, 1967), 82.
13. Martin Noth, *Leviticus,* trans. J. E. Anderson (Philadelphia: Westminster, 1965), 16.
14. Williams, *Bond That Breaks,* 66, and Bailey, *Homosexuality,* 60, as cited in Williams.
15. Bailey, *Homosexuality,* 60.
16. Williams, *Bond That Breaks,* 165, note 81.
17. N. H. Snaith, ed., *Leviticus and Numbers, New Century Bible* (London: Nelson, 1967), 125.
18. Letha Scanzoni and Virginia Mollenkott, *Is The Homosexual My Neighbor? Another Christian View* (San Francisco: Harper and Row, 1978), 59-60, 61.

## 5. The New Testament and Homosexuality

1. C. F. Peter Coleman, *Christian Attitudes To Homosexuality* (London: SPCK, 1980), 88. Williams, *The Bond That Breaks: Will Homosexuality Split the Church?* (Los Angeles: BIM, 1978), 70-71.
2. Williams, *Bond That Breaks,* 71; D. S. Bailey, *Homosexuality and the Western Christian Tradition* (London: Longmans, Green and Co., 1955), 27.
3. Victor Paul Furnish, *The Moral Teaching of Paul* (Nashville: Abingdon Press, 1979), 74; Robert A. Spivey and D. Moody Smith, *Anatomy of the New Testament,* 3rd ed. (New York: Macmillan, 1982), 360-61.
4. Robin Scroggs, *The New Testament and Homosexuality* (Philadelphia: Fortress Press, 1983), especially 23-26.
5. John J. McNeill, *The Church and the Homosexual* (Kansas City: Sheed Andrews and McMeel, 1976), 42.
6. Williams, *Bond That Breaks,* 114-20.
7. Hanz Conzelmann, *I Corinthians,* (Philadelphia: Fortress, 1975), 106; C. K. Bar-

rett, *A Commentary on the First Epistle to the Corinthians* (New York: Harper and Row, 1968), 140; Williams, *Bond That Breaks,* 82.

8. *See* Richard F. Lovelace, *Homosexuality and the Church* (Old Tappan: Fleming H. Revell, 1978), 96-97.
9. Williams, *Bond That Breaks,* 85.
10. John Boswell, *Christianity, Social Tolerance and Homosexuality: Gay People in Western Europe from the Beginning of the Christian Era to the Fourteenth Century* (Chicago: University of Chicago Press, 1980).
11. McNeill, *Church and the Homosexual,* 200, note 42.
12. Furnish, *Moral Teaching,* 72-73.
13. Williams, *Bond That Breaks.* 86.
14. Ibid.
15. Letha Scanzoni and Virginia Mollenkott, *Is The Homosexual My Neighbor? Another Christian View* (San Francisco: Harper and Row, 1978), 70.
16. Furnish, *Moral Teaching,* 78-82.

## 6. A Contemporary Debate on Homosexuality in the Church

1. John Calvin, *Institutes of the Christian Religion,* vol. 20 of The Library of Christian Classics, ed. J. T. McNeill, trans. Ford Lewis Battles (Philadelphia: Westminster Press, 1960), 35.
2. John Wesley, "Original Sin," sermon 38 in *Wesley's Standard Sermons,* vol. 2, 4th edition, 1955, ed. E. H. Sugden (Grand Rapids: Francis Asbury Press, 1988), 207-25; John Calvin, *Institute,* Book Two, chapter 2, 241-55; Martin Luther, "Lectures on Galatians," 1535, in *Luther's Works,* vol. 27, ed. Jaroslav Peli Kan, trans. Walter Hansen (St. Louis: Concordia Publishing House, 1963), 165-79.
3. *See* Eugene H. Peters, *Hartshorne and Neoclassical Metaphysics: and Interpretation* (Lincoln: University of Nebraska Press, 1970), especially chapter 5. Also, John B. Cobb, Jr. and David Ray Griffin, *Process Theology: An Introductory Exposition* (Philadelphia: Westminster Press, 1976), chapter 3, especially 47-48.
4. *See* Schubert Ogden, *The Reality of God* (New York: Harper and Row, 1966).
5. Ogden, *Faith and Freedom: Toward a Theology of Liberation* (Nashville: Abingdon, 1979), 47, 48.
6. *See* Frederick M. Herzog, *Justice Church: The New Function of the Church in North American Christianity* (New York: Orbis Books, 1980); James H. Cone, *Black Theology and Black Power* (New York: Seabury Press, 1969); Jose Miguez Bonino, *Doing Theology in a Revolutionary Situation* (Philadelphia: Fortress Press, 1975).
7. *See* John Patton, *Pastoral Counseling: A Ministry of the Church* (Nashville: Abingdon, 1983), 48.
8. *See* Gustavo Gutierrez, *The Mystical and Political Dimensions of the Christian Faith,* ed. C. Geffe and G. Gutierrez (New York: Herder and Herder, 1974); Ruben Alves, *A Theology of Human Hope* (Washington: Corpus Books, 1969).
9. John J. McNeill, *The Church and the Homosexual* (Kansas City: Sheed Andrews and McMeel, 1976), 109-25.
10. Philip Rieff, *Freud: The Mind of the Moralist* (Chicago: University of Chicago Press, 1979).
11. Sigmund Freud, *New Introductory Lectures* (Norton: New York, 1932). Other theorists in the psychological tradition are Erik Erikson, *Childhood and Society* (Norton: New York, 1950); Harry Stack Sullivan, *Interpersonal Theories of Psychiatry*

(Norton: New York, 1953). *See also* Jay R. Greenberg and Stephen A. Mitchell, *Object Relations and Psychoanalytic Theory* (Boston: Harvard, 1983) for an excellent discussion on the psychoanalytic school of psychology.

12. For a thorough presentation of the history of the debate of developmental versus innate causes of homosexuality, *see* David F. Greenberg, *The Construction of Homosexuality* (Chicago: University of Chicago Press, 1988), especially "Epilogue: Under the Sign of Sociology," 482-500. The debate of essentialist (innate) versus constructionist (developmental) is presented in this comparative approach to understanding the scope and variety of settings in which homosexuality occurs.

13. Ronald Bayer, *Homosexuality and American Psychiatry* (New York: Basic Books, 1981), 3.

14. Bayer, *Homosexuality*, 9.

15. Ibid., 96.

16. Ibid., 113, 115.

17. Ibid., 124, 128. *See* Robert L. Spitzer, "A Proposal About Homosexuality and the APA Nomenclature: Homosexuality as an Irregular Form of Sexual Development, and Sexual Orientation Disturbance as a Psychiatric Disorder," mimeographed. The Symposium on Homosexuality in the *Journal of American Psychiatric Association* (November 1973) suggests incorrectly that Spitzer's proposal was read at May 1973 panel. He only moderated the panel.

18. Ibid., 141. Robert Goldstein, "Letter," *Psychiatric News* (3 April, 1974), 2.

19. Ibid., 148.

20. Jonas Robitscher, as quoted in Bayer, *Homosexuality*, p. 165.

21. *DSM-III*, draft, December 20, 1977, L1, as quoted in Bayer, *Homosexuality*, 176.

22. *DSM-III*, draft, December 20, 1977, L2, as quoted in Bayer, *Homosexuality*, 177.

23. Richard F. Lovelace, *Homosexuality and the Church* (Old Tappan, N.J.: Fleming H. Revell, 1978), 29-63.

24. Lovelace, *Homosexuality and the Church*, 30.

25. *Journal of the General Convention of the Protestant Episcopal Church in the United States of America—otherwise known as the Episcopal Church* (New York: The General Convention Episcopal Church Center, 1979), C-88-9.

26. Harmon L. Smith, "Decorum as Doctrine: ECUSA's Recent Teachings on Human Sexuality" (unpublished paper, 1990), 14.

27. "News: United Presbyterian Church: Deciding the Homosexual Issue," in *Christianity Today* 23 (June 23, 1978), 38-41.

28. Anita Bryant, *The Anita Bryant Story* (Old Tappan, N.J.: Fleming H. Revell, 1977), especially chapter 11, "The Militant Homosexual."

29. *The Book of Discipline of The United Methodist Church*, 1984 (Nashville: The United Methodist Publishing House, 1984), 189.

30. Thomas Furman Hewitt, *The American Church's Reaction to the Homophile Movement, 1948-1978*. (Ph.D. diss., Duke University, 1983), 348-361; *see* Chart I: Denominational Statements, 348.

31. A. B. Simpson, *Days of Heaven on Earth* (Grand Rapids: Francis Asbury Press, reissue of the original 1897 edition in 1987), September 3 reading.

32. "Gay Lobbyist Reminds Hatch of Fund-Raiser," *Durham Morning Herald* (September 3, 1988), 5B.

33. Nicholas von Hoffman, *Citizen Cohn* (New York: Doubleday, 1988), 23, 27, 363.

34. Christopher Hitchens, "It Dare Not Speak Its Name: Fear and Self-Loathing on The Gay Right," *Harper's Magazine* 275 (August 1987), 72.

## 7. Homosexuality and the Church's Ministry

1. Darlene K. Bogle, "What If I Were Gay?" *Moody Monthly* (June 1985), 92.
2. Quoted in Randy Frame, "The Homosexual Lifestyle: Is There a Way Out?" *Christianity Today* 29 (August 9, 1985), 33.
3. Elizabeth R. Moberly, *Homosexuality: A New Christian Ethic* (Cambridge: James Clarke, 1983), 2. Also see "The Homosexual Lifestyle: Is There a Way Out?" *Christianity Today* 29 (August 9, 1985), 33.
4. "On Being Too Harsh," Park Avenue United Methodist *Church Bulletin*, Minneapolis, December 5, 1982, 4.
5. John E. Fortunato, *Embracing the Exile: Healing Journeys of Gay Christians* (New York: Seabury Press, 1983), especially chapter 9, "Exile For All: An Invitation."
6. *The Book of Discipline* (Nashville: The United Methodist Publishing House, 1984), "Social Principles," 90.
7. Bishop Earl Hunt, "On Being Leaders and Selecting Battle Lines," address to the Standing Committee on Pastoral Concerns, Council of Bishops, United Methodist Church, November 18, 1987, 11.
8. Ronald J. Sider, "AIDS: An Evangelical Perspective," *The Christian Century* (January 6-13, 1988), 11-14.
9. Earl Shelp, Ronald Sunderland, Peter W. A. Mansell, *AIDS: Personal Stories in Pastoral Perspective* (New York: Pilgrim Press, 1986).
10. Earl E. Shelp and Ronald Sunderland, *Handle with Care: A Handbook for Care Teams Serving People with AIDS* (Nashville: Abingdon, 1990).
11. Sider, "Evangelical Perspective," 13.
12. Andrés Tapia, "High-risk Ministry," *Christianity Today* (August 7, 1987), 18.
13. Robert N. Bellah *et al.*, *Habits of the Heart* (Berkeley: University of California Press, 1985).
14. David Aikman reports: "In a well-known survey of 216 leading U.S. journalists, conducted in 1981 by sociologists S. Robert Lichter and Stanley Rothman, 54 percent of the respondents thought adultery was not wrong, 75 percent considered homosexuality an acceptable lifestyle, 86 percent seldom or never went to church or synagogue, and 90 percent thought abortion was an inherent right of women." "The Press Is Missing the Scoop of the Century," *Christianity Today* (March 4, 1988), 12.

## 8. Intimacy, Vulnerability, and Sexuality

1. Sigmund Freud, *Three Essays on the Theory of Sexuality*, trans. James Strachey (London: Hogarth Press, 1962). *See also The Sexual Enlightenment of Children* (New York: Collier Books, 1963).
2. Paul A. Mickey, *Sex with Confidence: How to Achieve Physical and Emotional Intimacy in the New Sexual Age* (New York: William Morrow, 1988), 227.
3. M. Scott Peck, *The Road Less Traveled* (New York: Simon and Schuster, 1978), especially Section II: "Love," 81-182.
4. Harry Stack Sullivan, *Conceptions of Modern Psychiatry* (New York: W. W. Norton, 1953), 42-43.

# BIBLIOGRAPHY

Atkinson, David. *Homosexuals in the Christian Fellowship.* Grand Rapids: William B. Eerdmans, 1979.

Bailey, Derrick S. *Homosexuality and the Western Christian Tradition.* London: Longmans, Green and Co., 1955.

Barnhouse, Ruth and Urban T. Holmes, eds. *Male and Female Christian Approaches to Sexuality.* New York: Seabury Press, 1976.

Bayer, Ronald. *Homosexuality and American Psychiatry.* New York: Basic Books, 1981.

Bell, Alan and Martin S. Weinberg, eds. *Homosexuality: An Annotated Bibliography.* New York: Harper and Row, 1972.

Bell, Alan, M. Weinberg and G. Hammersmith, *Sexual Preference.* Bloomington: Indiana University Press, 1981.

Bergler, Edmund. *Homosexuality: Disease or Way of Life?* New York: Hill and Wang, 1957.

Diamant, Louis. *Male and Female Homosexuality: Psychological Approaches.* Washington: Hemisphere Publishing, 1987.

Edwards, George R. *Gay/Lesbian Liberation.* New York: Pilgrim Press, 1984.

Endleman, Robert. *Psyche and Society.* New York: Columbia University Press, 1981. *See* pp. 233-338.

Field, David. *The Homosexual Way: A Christian Option?* Bramcote Notts: Grove Books, 1976.

Fortunato, John E. *Embracing the Exile.* New York: Seabury Press, 1983.

Furnish, Victor. *The Moral of Teaching Paul.* Nashville: Abingdon Press, 1979.

Gramick, Jeannine, ed. *Homosexuality and the Christian Church.* Chicago: Thomas More, 1983.

Ide, Arthur F. *The City of Sodom*. Dallas: Monument Press, 1985.

Leopold, Kathleen, ed. *Theological Pastoral Resources*. Washington: Dignity Inc., 1981.

McNeill, John J. *The Church and the Homosexual*. Kansas City: Sheed Andrews and McMeel, 1976.

Marmor, Judd. *Homosexual Behavior*. New York: Basic Books, 1980.

*Ministry and Homosexuality in the Archdiocese of San Francisco*. San Francisco: Senate of Priests, 1983.

Moberly, Elizabeth R. *Homosexuality: A New Christian Ethic*. Cambridge: James Clark and Co., 1983.

Moss, Rachel, ed. *God's Yes to Sexuality*. London: British Council of Churches, 1981.

Nelson, James B. *Embodiment: An Approach to Sexuality and Christian Theology*. Minneapolis: Augsburg, 1978.

Nouwen, Henri. *Intimacy*. Indiana: Fides Publisher Inc., 1969.

Nugent, Robert, Jeannine Gramick, and Thomas Oddo, eds. *Homosexual Catholics: A New Primer for Discussion*. Washington: Dignity Inc., 1980.

Pittenger, Norman. *The Meaning of Being Human*. New York: The Pilgrim Press, 1982.

————. *Unbounded Love: God and Man in Process*. New York: Seabury, 1976.

Scanzoni, Letha and Virginia Mollenkott. *Is The Homosexual My Neighbor?* New York: Harper & Row, 1978.

Treese, Robert L. *Homosexuality: A Contemporary View of the Biblical Perspective*. Prepared for the Consultation on Theology and the Homosexual. Sponsored by Glide Urban Center and The Council on Religion and the Homosexual in San Francisco, August 22-24, 1966.

Van den Aardweg, Gerard. *On Origins and Treatment of Homosexuality*. New York: Praeger Publishing, 1986.

Williams, Don. *The Bond that Breaks: Will Homosexuality Split the Church?* Los Angeles: BIM, 1978.